ONE STEP MORE:

The Life and Work of
Father Joseph C. Martin

ONE STEP MORE:

The Life and Work of
Father Joseph C. Martin

JANE MAHER

ISBN 0-9661760-0-6 (hardcover)
ISBN 0-9661760-1-4 (paperback)

To order additional copies of this book, please contact:
Father Martin's Ashley
800 Tydings Lane
Havre de Grace, Maryland 21078
(410) 273-6600
1-800-799-HOPE (4673)
Fax: (410) 272-5617

All proceeds from the sale of this book will be used to support the
Ashley Scholarship Fund, a fund established to cover the expenses of
those who could otherwise not afford to be treated at Ashley.

For Mae Abraham,
who always seems to have more to give

Father Martin once asked Austin Ripley, the founder of Guest House, "How far do you go to help an alcoholic?" Ripley replied, "As far as you can, and then one step more."

Nothing we do, however virtuous, can be accomplished alone; therefore, we must be saved by love.

—Reinhold Niebuhr

INTRODUCTION

*I*t is particularly fitting that the biography of Father Joseph C. Martin be published in 1998, for this is the year during which Father will celebrate his fiftieth anniversary as a priest, his fortieth anniversary of sobriety, and the fifteenth anniversary of the founding of Ashley.

Father Martin has devoted more than half his life to saving alcoholics and addicts, and he is known and respected throughout the world as one of the most knowledgeable and effective speakers in the field of alcoholism recovery. Thousands of recovering alcoholics and addicts in the United States and around the world have heard Father deliver the Chalk Talk on Alcohol, and many thousands more have seen Father deliver the Chalk Talk via videotape. Today, almost 30 years after it was filmed, experts and professionals still describe the Chalk Talk as one of the most effective and informative explanations of alcoholism and addiction in existence.

Thousands of other recovering alcoholics and addicts know Father Martin through Father Martin's Ashley, the recovery facility that he co-founded with Mae Abraham, located in Havre de Grace, Maryland. Ashley is one of the pre-eminent treatment centers in the United States; more than 10,000 patients and 25,000 family members have stayed at Ashley, benefitting not only from the most effective treatment methods available today, but from the presence of Father Martin himself, whose every word and action is based on the passionate belief in the innate dignity of every human being.

Those people who have heard Father deliver his Chalk Talk and those people who have spent time at Ashley have had the opportunity to learn about Father's own struggle with alcohol, his discovery of the Twelve Steps through Austin Ripley during his stay at Guest House, his friendship with Mae Abraham, and the way that Ashley came into existence as a result of that friendship.

However, until now, there has never been a full account of the story of Father Martin's extraordinary life and the even more extraordinary impact he has had on the field of alcoholism recovery. In recognition and celebration of Father's lifelong work and devotion to the field, the board of directors of Father Martin's Ashley decided to honor Father's life work by commissioning a biography that would offer a full portrait of this most remarkable man. All proceeds from the sale of this book will be used to support the Ashley Scholarship Fund, a fund established to cover the expenses of those who could otherwise not afford to be treated at Ashley.

In conducting research for this biography, I interviewed scores of people, all of whom cooperated fully and gave generously of their time. They are quoted here with permission. In addition, I spent countless hours with Father Martin and Mae Abraham. I learned much from them, especially about the power of love.

Jane Maher
Greenwich, Connecticut

CHAPTER ONE

A Wonderful and Secure Childhood

*F*ather Joseph Charles Martin was born in Baltimore, Maryland, on October 12, 1924, to Marie Joseph Miller Martin and James Andrew Martin; he was the fourth of seven children. Marie and James Martin, both of whom had been born in Baltimore, were not wealthy, nor were they well educated— neither had completed elementary school. They were, however, proud, hard-working, and intelligent, and they were determined to provide their children with opportunities they had not had. Their families had been in the United States for many years: James Martin's grandparents had come to the Baltimore area from County Clare, Ireland, and Marie Miller's great grandparents had immigrated to Pennsylvania from England and Germany.

While Marie Miller's childhood was a typical and happy one, James Martin's mother died when he was ten years old, and his father, who felt that he could not work as a blacksmith and raise his four sons at the same time, left James and his brothers in the care of James's Uncle Jim and Aunt Sarah. It was a crowded household: in addition to their own children and their nephews, Jim and Sarah Martin took in boarders. At one point there were four males in the household named James; they were referred to as big Jim, little Jim, old Jim, and young Jim. James Martin (little Jim) worked at whatever odd jobs he could find; when he was only ten years old he began to work at Poole's Foundry in

Marie Miller and James Martin, shortly before their marriage.
(Courtesy of Mrs. Frances Osborne.)

Woodbury, Maryland, wiping down machinery, using his wages to help his aunt and uncle with expenses.

By the time James Martin married Marie Miller, he was employed as a skilled tool and die maker at the Rustless Iron and Steel Company in Baltimore, Maryland. He quickly earned a reputation as a perfectionist; when there was a particularly important or demanding job to be done, it was routinely assigned to him. Except for a brief period during the Depression he was never unemployed; however, he worked brutally hard, leaving the house each morning at 5:00, and working half days on Saturdays. By the advent of World War II, James Martin was already considered a master machinist, designing molds and equipment to be used in the production of weapons. During the war, when the company was filling government orders for machine-gun barrels, other workers would crank out 13 barrels in one shift—all of which would be rejected, while he would produce only four—all of which would be accepted.

Large families were not unusual during the early part of the twentieth century, particularly in the section of North Baltimore known as Hampden where the Martins settled soon after they

2

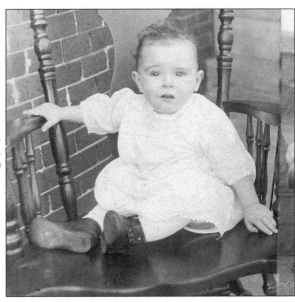

Joseph Martin in 1925.
(Courtesy of Mrs.
Dorothy Christopher.)

were married in June of 1914. Both James and Marie Martin were 28 at the time. Their first child, Leo, was born nine months after they were married, followed by Frances in 1917 and Marie in 1919. When Joseph was born in 1924, Frances, who was seven years old, adopted the role of "little mother"; in fact, it was she who chose Father Martin's name. (Father Martin was called Joe by practically everyone, except for Frances and his mother, who always called him Joseph.) Two years later, Edward was born; then in 1928, Bernard was born, followed two years later by the Martins' youngest child, Dorothy.

Leo, the oldest, was 16 when Dorothy was born; he was already preparing to enter college—one can only imagine the tenacity, patience, and devotion required to provide for each child at each stage of his or her life. "My mother never complained," Frances recalls.

> We were her pride and joy; it never occurred to
> her to be anything but a wife and mother. Cir-
> cumstances are different today of course, but
> when we were children growing up, everyone had

3

relatively large families, and my parents looked upon their children as a source of great happiness. We never felt unwanted or unloved; in fact, we were convinced that we were capable of anything, particularly academically. It was a wonderful and secure childhood.

When James and Marie Martin were raising their seven children their lives were, like the lives of many during that time period, guided by the belief that America was truly a land of opportunity. Almost everything parents did, they did for the sake of their children. Fathers worked to put food on the table while mothers stayed home to care for the children—there were no governmental safety nets in place, and taking charity was perceived as tantamount to admitting that one was an unfit provider. Parents scrimped and saved and struggled and sacrificed until they had put together enough money for a down payment on a house. Children were well loved—although there were far fewer outward manifestations of affection than are common today. It was not unusual for neighbors and other relatives to discipline children—not to do so would invoke criticism. But most important, everyone knew the value of education—it was the "ticket" out of poverty that parents dreamed of for their children.

The Martins lived in a typical brick, two-story, three-bedroom row house located at 805 Powers Street. They purchased it for 800 dollars in 1915, a huge sum at that time. (The house is still standing, and each time Father Martin walks past his childhood home, "it seems to get smaller and smaller.") As the family grew, the four boys shared the front bedroom, sleeping in two double beds, and the three girls shared another bedroom. Although the cost of raising seven children placed an enormous financial burden on James and Marie Martin, they were always able to provide the necessities. "We never went without food, nor did we have to stuff our shoes with newspaper," Father Martin recalls, "but we didn't have extras." In fact, Father wore hand-me-downs for his entire childhood. It wasn't until he was about to enter the seminary that he finally acquired clothes "that hadn't been worn

4

by someone else first." Edward recalls that during the Depression his mother would often make enormous pots of stew, serving half to her own large family and sending the other half across the alley to a family whose father was unemployed.

Although the Martins were not wealthy ("we were poor, but we didn't know it," Bernard recalls), and although there was the usual bickering among the children, it was a remarkably happy and secure environment, primarily because of Marie Martin's influence. Father still remembers how often his father would say, with great admiration, "Your mother is the greatest molder of character I know."

"She was always there," Frances recalls, "when we left for school in the morning, when we arrived home in the afternoon, when we went to bed at night. The children were the center of her life; she would do anything for us."

Father recalls that when he came home from school in the afternoon, his mother was often in the basement washing and hanging laundry—huge mounds of it—but "she was always happy to see us come home, stopping what she was doing to ask us about our day and to see that we changed into our play clothes and got a snack." Father also recalls that the children had no difficulty locating their mother when they arrived home from school: "We could always hear her humming."

Marie Martin found time, among the endless drudgery of cleaning, shopping, cooking, and doing laundry for a family of nine, to make every one of her children feel not only wanted, but special. From time to time, she would take one of the children aside and invite him or her to walk with her to Billy Burns's Confectionery Shop at 36th Street and Elm Avenue, just a few blocks from their house on Powers Street, to sit at the counter and enjoy an ice cream soda or some other treat. "Now don't tell the others about this," she would say to the child who was with her at the time. It wasn't until all of the children were adults that they discovered that each and every one of them had received the same warning.

The Martin children rarely got into trouble; Marie Martin saw to that. In fact, neighbors recall that the Martins "brought their children up the proper way," teaching them to respect others and to work hard. But Marie Martin didn't abide "snitches" either, Edward recalls. During the summer of his tenth year, he saw his brother Joe smoking a cigarette with a friend in an overgrown lot several blocks from their house. He ran all the way home to tell his mother what he had seen. "Don't you ever tattle on your brother again," Marie Martin told Edward, who was breathless and panting from his run. "She never said a word about the smoking to Joe," Edward recalls, "and needless to say, I never snitched on any of my brothers or sisters again."

But Marie Martin could also be a stern disciplinarian when she had to be. "She was raising seven children," Bernard recalls, "and she often had to put her foot down to maintain some semblance of order." Marie Martin established a routine that Father Martin still remembers to this day. "When we got home from school, we could go out and play, but then we'd all have to be in at a certain time for supper. We would sit around the supper table and eat our dinner together, every night, with rare exception. Then, after the table was cleared and the dishes were done, we children stayed at the table and did our homework." Although it was rare for girls to attend college during the 1920s and '30s, Marie Martin insisted that Marie, Frances, and Dorothy study as hard as their brothers. "Mother was as ambitious for the girls as she was for the boys," Dorothy remembers. "There were no double standards in our house."

Although Marie Martin taught her children to respect others, particularly adults, she also encouraged them to think for themselves. Frances still remembers discussions around the dining room table that were heated, interesting, and loud. "We were all good at expressing ourselves," she recalls, "and we had great confidence in our opinions—boy did we all like to talk."

All of the Martin children were intelligent and did well academically, an enormous source of pride to their parents. Educational achievement was recognized and admired on Powers

6

Street, as it was in all blue-collar neighborhoods; it replaced wealth as a barometer of success. Leo, the oldest, won full academic scholarships to high school, college, and graduate school. Father Martin remembers that long after the other children had gone to bed, Leo would remain at the dining room table, studying and reading. (He often earned perfect scores on standardized scholarship examinations.) Father remembers the pride and satisfaction his parents felt over Leo's accomplishments: everyone—neighbors, friends, relatives, and teachers—recognized his brilliance. He eventually became a highly respected research chemist.

Of the three girls, Marie was probably the feistiest. Like Father Martin, she had bright red hair, and Father remembers his mother telling Marie whenever they argued that she had better stop shaking her red head and pay attention to what her mother was saying. "It's my red head," Marie would reply; "I can shake it if I want to." Her mother would just frown and say, "Some day, young lady, you're going to get married and have children who are just like you!" Dorothy was, Father recalls, "as bright as a silver dollar. She could write poetry the way that most of us write prose, and she wrote poems about all of her siblings that we loved to hear recited."

Edward Martin, two years younger than Father, was nicknamed "the little professor," because he was always asking about everything, driving Leo crazy. "He was also very much like my mother," Father remembers. "He was the quietest of all the children, rarely offering an opinion unless you asked for it, but if you did ask for it, you got it!" Father Martin also remembers that "Edward had a sensitive conscience and lived by it."

Edward still recalls, more than 65 years later, the way that Father got Edward to pull him along the streets of their neighborhood in a small red cart. "You know the way Tom Sawyer convinced his friends that he was doing them a favor letting them whitewash the fence? Well, that's what Joe did to me—by the time he got through sweet talking me, I thought it was the greatest favor anyone could have done—letting me pull him along the street in a wagon!" In addition to Father's powers of persuasion, he was the yo-yo champion of the neighborhood, winning first prize (a sweater) from the proprietor of Burns's Confectionery Shop for performing a set of tricks better than any other contestant.

Father Martin was also well known in the neighborhood for his kindness. There was a young boy from a large family with such a serious speech impediment that none of the children ever quite figured out what to call him; as best they could decipher from his fractured speech, his name was Ducky Neal. Most of the children in the neighborhood, particularly the older boys, ridiculed him, but Father befriended the little boy instead. Frances remembers that Ducky came to the house many afternoons during the summer asking for her brother. If Joseph was home, he would greet Ducky, and then walk him home. With Father as an escort, Ducky could be assured safe passage past the group of boys who usually hung out on the corner. In fact, once it became apparent to the boys that Joseph Martin didn't ridicule Ducky's speech, they began to treat Ducky more gently, until the teasing stopped altogether.

On Sunday mornings, Marie Martin would attend Mass at their parish church, St. Thomas Aquinas, with her seven children in tow. More often than not, her husband did not attend, a source of sorrow and consternation for Marie. "Dad stayed away from church for many years," Father recalls, "and it was a very painful part of our lives, but our mother would never comment or criticize him about this in front of the children." Father remembers his father as

> a bit contrary. He just didn't like to be told what to do, and he didn't like to do things just because everyone else was doing them. If everyone was getting dressed up for an occasion, Christmas or Easter for example, he would get it into his head *not* to get dressed up. It makes me smile now to think about it, but at the time it was unpleasant and embarrassing, especially for my mother.

Then there was Aunt Mabel, Marie Martin's sister, who lived with the family for about six years. She worked in a factory and often contributed money to the household, but Father recalls,

> She just drove Dad crazy. She was older than my mother; she had never married, and she tried to dominate and control our family. Although she loved the children and we loved her, she often disciplined us, overriding or contradicting instructions our parents had given us, and she frequently demanded to know where my mother had been, why she had done something in a certain way. She would never let any of us leave the house without an umbrella—of course we just humored her and hid the umbrellas in the vestibule closet. She favored Leo because of his brilliance and decided that *he* should become a priest.

(More than 40 years later, when Father Martin delivered his first Chalk Talk, he used the name Mabel to refer to a particularly self-righteous type of non-drinker, one who "can't understand an addict because she isn't one herself," and described Mabel as one who "wakes up in the morning, looks at her hair in the mirror, says 'part,' and it does.")

There was another aunt who had an enormous influence on the children, Marie's other sister, Mary Louise. The children called her Aunt Luli, and although she didn't live with the Martins, she visited them a couple of times a week. On each visit, she brought toys and candy for the children. Aunt Mabel would scold her for indulging in such a foolish waste of money, but Aunt Luli paid no attention—as a result, the children loved her and looked forward to her visits. It's possible that Father Martin was Aunt Luli's favorite; Frances remembers that she gave him an Indian Head penny collection that he treasured.

The dominant impression that all of the Martin children have retained of their father is of a taciturn, hard-working man. "Even when he was home," Bernard recalls, "when he wasn't napping, he was always making repairs around the house." One particular memory that Father cherishes is of the patience, gentleness, and concern that his father showed toward Edward, who was born with a club foot. Father recalls how the family doctor explained to his father that Edward's foot would have to be worked and massaged in a certain way, for a certain amount of time, every day.

> No matter how tired my father was when he came home from work, he would do precisely what the doctor had told him to do. He would work Edward's foot every night before dinner. This went on for years and was part of the daily routine in the Martin house. And it worked. When Edward was in high school, he was on the junior varsity track team—no one would ever suspect that there had been a problem. Even the doctor was amazed.

(During the Depression, this same doctor hired James Martin to chauffeur him back and forth to the hospital. "That's what got us through those rough years," Father Martin recalls.)

Frances remembers the pride her father took in the fact that his wife did not have to tend to the furnace, as most women did. "In those days, we had furnaces into which the coal had to be shoveled. Daddy took care of that every morning before the rest of us got up, and he took care of it again at night before bedtime. He liked to say that his wife 'didn't know what the furnace looked like.'"

During the years that James and Marie Martin were struggling to raise seven children on a machinist's salary, no one knew very much about the disease of alcoholism. There were the neighborhood drunks, predominantly men, who would be seen staggering down the block during the daytime ("we knew them all by name," Father Martin recalls), and there were those, again mostly men, who would never miss a day's work but who would stop at a neighborhood bar after work; this is the category into which James Martin fell. "Dad didn't drink every night," Father recalls, he couldn't afford to. But he did drink two or three nights a week, spending money that my mother desperately needed at home. He worked hard and he drank hard. As we grew older, we began to be more critical of his behavior, but my mother wouldn't tolerate us criticizing our father, not even for a moment. "He's your father," she would say to us. "He works hard to provide for you. He has provided everything you have, and don't you forget it."

But that's not to say my mother didn't suffer as a result of his drinking. Those were difficult times, and many years later, after I had been ordained, my mother mentioned in one of her letters to me that perhaps she would talk to our parish priest about a trial separation. Of course, nothing ever came of it, but it does reflect her frustration at a terrible problem that did not go away. God bless her; she endured so much.

Frances remembers her mother's aversion to alcohol, a result, of course, of her husband's drinking: "My mother could smell alcohol from around the corner, and I can't tell you how many times she would say, with great distress, 'I hate alcohol like the devil hates holy water.'"

Frances remembers that her father often slept very late on Saturdays and Sundays, having come home from the bar late the night before. "It made it seem as if he wasn't around very much," Frances recalls:

He didn't get involved with our lives. He never came to see Bernard pitch, even though the ball field was only a few blocks away and Bernard was the star of his team. He never came with us on Sunday afternoons to visit Joseph when he was in the seminary, even though St. Mary's was only a 15-minute ride by streetcar. It would never occur to us to say anything to him, but we did notice

11

Mrs. Marie Martin, center, with
Frances, left, and Dorothy, right.
(Courtesy of Mrs. Dorothy Christopher.)

Front to back: Edward, Joseph, and Leo
in the cassocks they wore as altar boys.
(Courtesy of Mrs. Frances Osborne.)

the other fathers there, and although we didn't
admit it, it hurt us.

St. Thomas Aquinas Parish was, in many ways, the center of the
Martin family's life. Marie and James Martin had been married
there, the children had been baptized there, and the children
attended the parish grammar school. Father Martin still remembers the name of the nun—Sister Adelaide—who prepared him
and his six brothers and sisters to receive their first communion.
All seven Martin children were confirmed there as well. Leo,
Edward, Joseph, and Bernard served as altar boys at St. Thomas
Aquinas, a source of enormous pride for their parents. Father
Martin remembers the way his mother would wake him or one
of his brothers each morning at 5:45 to serve at the 6:30 Mass.
(Dorothy still remembers a favorite family story about Father
serving Mass as an altar boy one Christmas morning, when he
was about eight years old, wearing his favorite Christmas present—the toy double six-shooter guns in a holster around his
waist under his cassock.)

Even at that young age, however, Father's deep faith and love of his religion was evident. Dorothy recalls that he would listen again and again to stories about Christ as a child, and he was enormously proud to have been named after Saint Joseph.

Father was an excellent student. From the time he entered the first grade at St. Thomas Aquinas Elementary School in 1930 until he graduated in 1938, he was, Jack Anderson, his childhood friend, remembers, "always one of the smartest kids in the class of 33 students." In fact, Father Martin and Jack Anderson were often competitors, albeit friendly ones, along with two girls, Betsy Reilly and Mary Reynolds, with whom they competed for top honors throughout all eight years of elementary school. Jack Anderson remembers that neighborhoods were extremely "stable" in those days; it wasn't uncommon for the same children who began their education together in the first grade to graduate together eight years later.

Like just about everyone who knew Father Martin during those years, Jack Anderson remembers Father's extraordinary sense of humor, his wonderful ability to tell good stories, and his generosity. "Material things weren't very important to him; he'd give something away if someone else wanted it. I think Joe had already begun to think about the priesthood at that time. He was a serious student, particularly in Religion class, and he admired the School Sisters of Notre Dame enormously. Although he cut up a bit in class, he was never disrespectful, and it was clear that he was one of the sisters' favorites because of this, and because of his intelligence."

Father's brothers and sisters still remember his extraordinary good nature. He loved to tell jokes and stories, and even at a young age, he was an accomplished mimic. He was, Frances recalls, "as outgoing as a politician. He was a good listener, and he was a great conversationalist." "Joe genuinely liked people," Edward recalls. "He didn't smooth talk people—he really engaged in conversations with them; he seemed happy to be with them."

Children were expected to study and excel at St. Thomas Aquinas, but in a brochure that was prepared many years later to celebrate the thirtieth reunion of the eighth graders, the former students recorded their memories of many wonderful occasions as well: the yearly trips to Notre Dame of Maryland for the Children's Fair; the annual picnic for altar boys and choir members at Bay View Park; Father McGraw's Silver Jubilee Celebration when the boys, wearing black suits and top hats, sang "How do you do Father McGraw, how are you?" while the girls, dressed as flowers, danced; the annual carnivals and hay rides; when the students, second graders at the time, had to stand until they all knew the multiplication tables; and "when someone released a 'stink bomb' in Sister Cordelia's class, and she made all the students stand around the room until the one who did it owned up."

Almost 60 years later, Jack Anderson still remembers the eighth-grade elocution contest held to determine which student would represent St. Thomas Aquinas School in an archdiocesan competition for a scholarship to Loyola High School.

> Joe was an excellent speaker. He could speak extemporaneously better than anyone I've known, but I was a pretty good speaker myself, and he and I were the two school finalists. Joe was chosen to represent the school, and he went on to win the archdiocese-wide contest. As a result, he was awarded a full scholarship to Loyola.

Loyola was (and still is) an all-male, highly selective Jesuit high school located in Towson, Maryland, an affluent suburb of Baltimore. "With anyone else," Jack Anderson recalls, "I suppose I would have been jealous, but with Joe, you just knew he deserved to win, and he was modest and gracious about it." Jack Anderson had also been accepted by Loyola High School, and his friendship with Father would continue for the next four years and beyond.

The Anderson family was a bit better off than the Martin family, but wealth had not been a very important factor during the elementary-school years; tuition at St. Thomas Aquinas was 50 cents per month per child, and if a family could not afford to pay it, the parish often waived the fee. As a freshman at Loyola High School in 1938, however, Father Martin began to realize, for the first time in his life, that his family had less money than many of the other boys' families did. Although the Martins would not have to pay tuition at Loyola, they had other tuition to pay (all three girls attended Seton High School, run by the Sisters of Charity), along with books, carfare, and clothing. It was a difficult time for them financially. Dorothy remembers that although they managed, "I could see that my parents, particularly my mother, felt the strain of providing for us. She never wanted us to feel deprived, but she couldn't give us as much as she would have liked."

Father remembers that he "began to notice the other boys had better clothes, and more of them. They also had spending money. I suppose I felt a bit out of place as a result, but the other boys seemed to accept me as I was, so after a while I didn't give it much thought."

Actually, within the first few weeks of classes, Father became one of the most popular members of the freshman class; his financial status quickly became irrelevant as the other boys recognized and were drawn to his wit, his friendliness, and his ability to tell funny stories.

Father did not let his popularity interfere with his schoolwork, however. His brother Leo had attended Loyola High School before him, and he was determined to maintain the family reputation—and be worthy of his scholarship. Father Martin's transcripts from his four years at Loyola High School reflect high intelligence and intellectual curiosity. His lowest grade during all four years of an exceedingly rigorous curriculum was an 84 in Greek Literature during his sophomore year. Most of his other grades were in the high eighties and nineties: in Algebra, Latin Composition and Literature, English Composition and Literature, History, Christian Doctrine, and French. At the end of his sophomore year, Father elected to major in the classics rather than the sciences, so he was required to take only one year of Biology during his senior year. (Although Father "never understood the sciences," he earned a grade of 87 in the course.)

Father still remembers one incident that occurred at the end of his first year at Loyola High School that caused him "much pain and embarrassment."

Father had a small part in a dramatic performance, and he was surprised when his father arrived in the auditorium, having come straight from work to see his son perform. He was still in his work clothes, Father recalls,

> and he smelled of grease and oil from the plant, and of whiskey from the bar. He got into a conversation with one of the teachers, Mr. Comey, who was preparing to become a Jesuit priest. They began to talk about educational issues, when suddenly my father said, "Yeah, we're told that our kids need a Catholic education, but it's only available to those who have enough money to send them."
>
> My brother Leo had already attended Loyola on a full scholarship, and I was now receiving the best possible education at Loyola High School—absolutely free, and here was my father, who had probably had too much to drink, complaining about the unfairness of it all to one of the teachers. I remember the mortification I felt; I hoped that no one else had heard my father. It was one of those moments when you suddenly recognize the frailties of those whom you've loved and trusted all your life—a painful moment. I'll never forget it.

By the end of his sophomore year, Father's ability to tell stories and to mimic accents and mannerisms had been refined to a point where he could speak and perform, extemporaneously, on practically any given topic. "Joe Martin was outstanding on the stage both as an actor and as a speaker," reads a 1941 entry in the

Loyola yearbook, the same year in which Father had a part in the school's production of Dickens' *Oliver Twist*.

Father had begun to develop a love for the theater; he would attend regional productions in and around Baltimore as often as he could afford the price of a ticket, inviting his brothers and his friends along. Edward still remembers when he and Father took their mother to see a production of *The Student Prince*. "We thought it was great," Edward recalls, "but Joe noticed everything about the production, and I am certain that he was learning from watching the actors deliver their lines."

The summer before Father's senior year at Loyola High School, he began to work full-time, from 3:30 p.m. to 11:00 p.m., at St. Mary's Seminary, located about two miles north of his home in Baltimore. Although Father had taken the job primarily to earn extra money, something else attracted him to the job: there were about 400 seminarians residing at the seminary, studying and training for the priesthood under the guidance of the Sulpician Fathers. "I loved the camaraderie of the priests and the students," Father recalls,

> and there was something about their dedication to God and to teaching that was very appealing to me. It seemed like such a meaningful way to live. There was no phoniness, no self-aggrandizement or self-promotion. These men had a calmness and a peacefulness about them that I had never seen before.

Late in the evening, when the switchboard was quiet, Father would often overhear the priests talking to the seminarians about their studies and about their future lives as priests. It was, Father now realizes, the early stirring of his own vocation to the priesthood.

The Sulpician priests (members of the Society of St. Sulpice, founded in France in 1641) had a long and special history in Baltimore. During the French Revolution, members of the Society were expelled from France. In 1791, John Carroll, the first Catholic bishop and head of the first diocese in the new world, invited the Sulpicians to Baltimore, where they founded St. Mary's Seminary—the first seminary to be established in the United States. The Sulpicians maintained a strong presence in Baltimore, and in 1941 the society celebrated its three-hundredth anniversary by hosting the largest gathering of American bishops in the history of the Catholic Church. At the time of the celebration, there were 12,000 priests in the United States who had been trained by the Sulpicians.

Father's primary responsibility was to cover the switchboard. The pay was ten dollars a week, and Marie Martin saved this money to be used for Father's college tuition. This meant that during the school year, Father began classes at 8:00 a.m., went straight to the seminary from Loyola High School, and got home at 11:30 at night. This didn't seem to bother him very much at all: "the work was easy enough," he recalls, and "there was plenty of free time at the switchboard to do my homework." Within a few months, Father's salary was increased to 11 dollars a week.

Father Martin did not let his busy schedule or his growing admiration for the Sulpician priests affect his high-school friendships. It was around this time, 1942, that Jack Anderson purchased his first car—a 1931 black Ford. The long, boring trip by streetcar and bus to Loyola High School was officially over: Jack Anderson and Father Martin, along with two other friends, Ed McGarry and Harry Shock, began to pool their money in order to put enough gas in the car ("a real guzzler," Jack Anderson recalls) to get to and from school. "In those days, we weren't ashamed to ask for 50 cents' worth of gas at the pump," notes Jack Anderson. "We had so much fun in that car, driving back and forth to school and an occasional trip to the shore. We couldn't have speeded even if we wanted to; the car was a real jalopy. But for four young boys to have a car to drive around Baltimore in 1942—we thought we were really something."

Loyola High School hosted an annual oratorical contest, and during his four years at Loyola, Father was awarded first place two times (he finished second the other two years). In addition, Father became a key member of Loyola's debating team, earning

"We loved riding around in my 1931 Ford," recalls Jack Anderson. (Courtesy of Mr. Jack Anderson.)

recognition from fellow students, teachers, and members of other teams.

Father was one of the school's lead debaters against teams from Jesuit high schools in New York, Philadelphia, and Washington. The teams were required to "declaim" over such political issues as labor legislation, and as World War II became more and more inevitable, whether the United States should join with Great Britain in a military alliance. Father Martin and his team, which called itself the Bellarmine Debating Society, were featured on a Baltimore radio station, WBAL (today the official station of the Baltimore Orioles), and Frances remembers that the entire Martin family gathered around the radio "to hear Joseph do over the airwaves precisely what he had been doing at home for years: convince people of the logic of his point of view."

Father Martin was never arrogant or pedantic, however; the 78-member senior class liked and admired him so much that, in addition to naming him the best debater, the best actor, and the member of the senior class with the best smile, they named him class valedictorian—an extraordinary honor.

Marie Martin never wanted to seem too proud of her children's accomplishments, but Frances remembers that on the evening of June 14, 1942, as she listened to her son speak to the

19

members of Loyola's graduating class and their teachers, family members, and friends, she glowed with pride and pleasure.

Father Martin spent the summer of 1942 working at the seminary, then in September of that year he began his first year at the all-male Loyola College, a Jesuit institution located on North Charles Street in Baltimore. Father used the money he had saved from his seminary job to pay his tuition.

Father was as popular in college as he had been in high school, but as he continued to work at St. Mary's Seminary, he began to feel more and more strongly the desire to enter the priesthood. There had been one young woman to whom he had felt an attraction during his senior year of high school, but his busy schedule had precluded anything ever coming of the relationship. He continued to sense that his life would not be like that of his classmates—the contemplative life held an attraction for him that his peers simply did not share or understand. One night, while performing his usual duties at the seminary, he entered the chapel to close the windows. As he knelt before the Blessed Sacrament in the still and quiet evening, Father asked God for guidance and knowledge: was his growing attraction to the priesthood a sign of a vocation? At that moment, he felt a great sense of calm and serenity, as if God had helped him, once and for all, to make the most important decision of his life.

Father Martin remained at Loyola College for two years; as usual, he excelled in the humanities: English and Speech, Latin, French, History, and particularly Philosophy (earning a grade of 93). But he still remembers the way Leo tried to help him prepare for final exams in Inorganic Chemistry and General Physics. Although Father Martin passed both courses, he "never understood a word my professors or Leo said." Despite this difficulty, Father ranked in the top third of his freshman and sophomore class at Loyola College.

He never felt, however, the same camaraderie and sense of fun that he had enjoyed at Loyola High School. This had more to do with his growing conviction that he wanted to prepare for the priesthood than with the college. As a result, after consulting with

Father Philip Hannan, a priest who had been assigned to St. Thomas Aquinas Parish two years earlier, and after discussing his decision with his parents and with the priests at St. Mary's Seminary, Father Martin decided to begin training for the priesthood.

There was never any question about which seminary he would attend: although he admired the Jesuits enormously, Father valued even more the example that had been set by the Sulpician priests during the three years he had worked at the switchboard at St. Mary's Seminary: men who were dedicated to their own spiritual and intellectual growth as well as that of their students.

The Sulpicians have been described as "the most learned of the Catholic communities of men." The society had originated in France, and many of its early members had been educated at the Sorbonne. Members of the Society of St. Sulpice have often been described as "priest's priests," because their exclusive mission is to train and educate seminarians who will then return to their own diocese after ordination to serve as parish priests. However, Father Martin did not intend to serve the Diocese of Baltimore; he wanted to join the Sulpician congregation itself so that he too could some day instruct seminarians.

Father Martin knew he was choosing a life that would be lonely and challenging at times—and that he would be forfeiting the joy and companionship of marriage and children. But throughout his five years of spiritual and intellectual training, years of great difficulty and sacrifice, Father remembered and was inspired by something one of the priests in the seminary had told him: "We insult the young by never asking of them the gigantic sacrifices of which they are capable."

CHAPTER TWO

❦

Getting Rid of the Empties

*F*ather Martin began his preparation for the priesthood at St. Mary's Seminary on Paca Street in central Baltimore in 1944. He remained there for two years, along with 200 other seminarians, completing the equivalent of an undergraduate degree in philosophy. (During the two years that Father Martin had attended Loyola College, most of the other seminarians had been enrolled at St. Charles College, in Baltimore, a minor seminary run by the Sulpicians.)

Those seminarians who successfully completed the two years of training in philosophy at Paca Street continued their training in Theology at St. Mary's Roland Park, located in north Baltimore. Under ordinary circumstances, seminarians remained at the Roland Park facility for four years, but because of World War II, summer vacations were shortened in order to reduce the length of study to three years. Seminarians were granted exemption from service in the armed forces.

Father Martin and the other seminarians at St. Mary's Paca Street learned about the founder of the Sulpician Society, Jean-Jacques Olier, the enormous sacrifices he made to establish the Society of Saint Sulpice (named after a parish in Paris, France), and the spiritual goals he set for all those seminarians who would follow him. "The first and ultimate end of this institute," Olier wrote in 1650,

> is to live supremely for God, in Christ Jesus our
> Lord, in order that the interior disposition of His

> Son may so penetrate the very depths of our
> heart, that each may say what St. Paul confident-
> ly affirmed of himself, "I live, but it is not I who
> live but it is Christ who liveth in me!" Such shall
> be the sole hope of all, their sole meditation, their
> sole exercise, to live the life of Christ interiorly,
> and to manifest it exteriorly in their mortal body.

In addition to their studies, Father Martin and the other seminarians engaged in rigorous spiritual training that included reading scripture, praying the rosary, devotion to the Blessed
Sacrament, weekly confession, daily Mass, spiritual direction,
conferences with the rector, and private prayer.

When Father arrived at St. Mary's Seminary to begin his
preparation for the priesthood, he already felt very much at
home: he had worked at Roland Park for more than three years;
he knew (and was well liked by) the Sulpician priests who would
now become his teachers; and most important, he was only a few
miles from home. Frances and Dorothy still remember the prepa-
rations Marie Martin conducted to get her son ready to "leave"
for the seminary. "She bought Joe all new clothes," Dorothy
remembers, "right down to his underwear and socks. You'd think
he was leaving for some faraway mission in China the way she
fussed over him." Frances recalls her mother's pride at the
prospect of having a son who might become a priest.

> Particularly in those days, it was every Catholic
> mother's dream. Mother would never push one of
> the boys to enter the priesthood, however.
> Edward had studied at St. Mary's for a very short
> time before deciding that he didn't have a voca-
> tion, and Mother did everything she could to
> assure Edward that she respected his decision to
> leave. But when it became apparent that Joseph
> was comfortable with his vocation, Mother
> couldn't hide her pleasure.

Father still remembers that his mother would ask him from
time to time if he still felt he had made the right decision.

Left to right: Father Ed Carr, Bernard, Dorothy, Edward, Mrs. Marie Martin, and Father Martin, circa 1945. (Courtesy of Father Martin.)

"Joseph," she would say, "don't think that you have to stay in the seminary for my sake. If you ever feel you want to leave, come home."

During the two years that the seminarians resided at St. Mary's on Paca Street, a five-story brick building surrounded by a high brick wall topped with shards of broken glass, the seminarians often joked that the glass wasn't intended to keep intruders out, it was intended to keep them in. There was a courtyard about the size of a square city block where the boys could play ball, but they actually had very little free time to do so.

The seminarians quickly grew comfortable in their new surroundings, but Frances remembers thinking that her brother was living in "the dungeon of the world, with its dark rooms, its big, heavy, dark furniture, a cemetery on the grounds for Sulpician priests. It just loomed there like something out of *Wuthering Heights*." To this day, Frances is sure that the young men who arrived by cab from the airport and saw the seminary for the first time, "must have been tempted to climb back into the cab and go back home." Father Martin remembers, however, that "it didn't take long for the spirit of the place to take effect; by the time the two years had ended, most of the seminarians were

*Father Martin with his parents
in their backyard, circa 1945.
(Courtesy of Father Martin.)*

reluctant to leave Paca Street for the new facilities at Roland Park."

Whether the building was as foreboding as Frances describes, there is no doubt that the other seminarians were homesick, at least initially; for many of them, it was their first prolonged period of time away from their parents and siblings, and the all-male environment at St. Mary's did little to replace the comforts they had enjoyed at home. As a result, Marie Martin made it clear that Joseph should bring his fellow seminarians home with him on free days. The seminarians had very little time to themselves, but they were always granted the days after Christmas and Easter off.

Dorothy remembers that on the actual holiday, her mother would prepare a big dinner for the Martin family: turkey, vegetables, fruit pies for dessert. Very often, there would be "enough leftovers to feed an army." However, on the very next day, when Father and two or three of his classmates were due to visit, Dorothy would hear her mother in the kitchen at 6:00 in the morning preparing another feast from scratch. When Dorothy asked her mother why she didn't serve the leftovers, Marie Martin grew indignant: "I would never do such a thing," she replied. "These boys are away from home and family on the holidays. This is the least I can do." Frances and Dorothy began to tease their mother, accusing her of preparing a better meal for the seminarians than for her own family.

And then there was the issue of laundry. By this time, Dorothy had begun to take on more and more of the household chores, and the first time she and Frances brought their brother's laundry home from the seminary, she simply added it to the family wash. "My mother was aghast when she saw what I was doing," Dorothy recalls. "You've got to wash Joseph's clothes separately," Marie Martin insisted. When Dorothy asked why, her mother explained that his clothing couldn't be mixed with James Martin's work clothes. "Well then," Dorothy inquired, "why is it okay for my clothes to be mixed with Daddy's work clothes?"

"Just do as I say," Marie Martin retorted. From that moment on, both Father and Marie Martin were teased mercilessly about the "sacred wash."

In addition to picking up and dropping off their brother's laundry, it was also Frances and Dorothy's duty to take the streetcar from home to the Paca Street seminary to bring food to their brother. "Mother seemed to think that Joseph was starving," Frances recalls. Marie Martin's reputation as an excellent cook soon spread among the seminarians. "We started getting requests for this or that," Frances recalls. "And mother was only too happy to oblige."

Father was as popular and well liked in the seminary as he had been during high school and the two years he spent at Loyola College. Father John Olivier had begun his studies two years before Father Martin, and he remembers Father Martin's arrival:

> Joe had a very attractive personality, and it was easy to like him. There was his humor of course; everyone loved his jokes and imitations, and he was admired for his ability not only to see the humor in things but to use humor to make his point. But his popularity was based on something far more substantial than that. Joe had a beautiful, sweet simplicity about him that made us want to be around him. Even our professors, who were

27

supposed to maintain some sense of authority and distance from us, could not help laughing at Joe's jokes or smiling at his good humor and countenance.

Father Martin loved to sing, and he had an excellent voice. Father John Selner was the choir director, and after an audition, Father was accepted as a member of the seminary choir. One of Father's most special memories of the years he spent as a seminarian was the annual Midnight Mass: "We made the most beautiful music—for the honor and glory of God of course—and it gave us men great pleasure."

Father soon realized, however, the depth of the sacrifices he would be required to make as a priest.

> There were many rules that we had to follow, rules that made perfect sense in terms of our training and preparation, but that were very difficult for me. I finally went to my confessor, Father John Sullivan, and I told him how I was feeling; the schedule of study, prayer, and silence was unrelenting. Because of the war, our four-year program of study was being condensed to three, and as a result our summer vacations were cut to two weeks.
>
> Father Sullivan let me go on for a while with my moaning and groaning, and then he said to me, very simply: "Joe, what in heaven's name do you think the priesthood is all about?" I've never forgotten that. Those words have gotten me through almost 50 years as a Sulpician priest. I came to realize that while variety may be the spice of life, monotony and routine are the essence of life.

One could not blame Father Martin for complaining. Training for seminarians during the 1940s and '50s, when vocations were at their height in the United States, was rigorous and unrelenting. The seminarians rose each day at 5:40; morning prayer and meditation began at 6:00, followed by Mass. On certain days of the week during lunch and dinner—throughout which the seminarians were required to maintain silence—one of the students would read, usually from a spiritual book.

After 7:30 breakfast, there were three class periods, followed by prayer in the chapel. After lunch the seminarians were given a short period of recreation; when the weather permitted, they usually congregated in the courtyard, talking and laughing for a half hour before afternoon classes began. At the end of afternoon classes, the young men would have another half-hour recreation period until 5:40, when they would pray the rosary individually, in silence. At 6:00 there would be a spiritual conference convened by the rector.

After supper, there was another short recreation period. Evening prayers began promptly at 7:30, followed by study time. From the time study period began at 7:30 until the next morning when breakfast was served, the seminarians were not permitted to speak; Father still remembers that the seminarians referred to this rule as "The Great Silence."

In addition to study and prayer, there were "house jobs" assigned once a year by the faculty, and each seminarian was assigned chores. Father Martin remembers that he was a head waiter during one of his years at the seminary. The least popular seminarian at any given time was usually the one who was the "regulator" whose duty it was to ring the wake-up bell each morning.

Although lifelong friendships were formed during these years of study and preparation, the seminarians were forbidden to become too close or to spend too much time together. The young men could talk to each other when the rule of silence was not being enforced, but they were never permitted to enter each other's rooms. At all times, a seminarian had to have at least one foot in the hallway. Such discipline was deemed essential, and the seminarians did not question the authority of their superiors. The Second Vatican Council would not occur for another 20 years:

seminarians who could not—or would not—abide by the strict rules had no choice but to leave St. Mary's.

The move from Paca Street to the seminary at Roland Park marked an extraordinary change for the young men. Roland Park was (and still is) a beautiful, pastoral setting, particularly in contrast to the Paca Street building and grounds. The small courtyard enclosed by a high brick wall topped with glass shards at Paca Street was replaced by 175 acres of rolling lawns and trees, surrounded by a tall, neatly trimmed hedge. The rooms were large and well lit (Father remembers the "luxury" of a sink in each room), and the terrazzo-tiled floors in the halls and foyers of Roland Park lent the seminary an air of European grandeur.

There were about 400 seminarians from 55 American dioceses and several countries and 30 faculty members at Roland Park during the time Father Martin completed his training from 1945 to 1948—and the rules of silence and discipline were as strictly enforced at Roland Park as they had been at Paca Street.

However, the academic curriculum was even more rigorous than it had been at Paca Street. In fact, the Sulpician seminaries in the United States were among the first to receive accreditation from such secular agencies as the Middle States Association. At Roland Park the seminarians engaged in scriptural exegesis and the study of dogmatic and moral theology, Scripture, homiletics (the act of preparing sermons and of preaching), and canon law. Father still remembers the four volumes of Moral Theology assigned to the seminarians.

> Our textbooks were written by a Sulpician, Father Adolphe Tanquerey, and those volumes, along with the teachings of St. Thomas Aquinas, provided me with such intellectual stimulation and pleasure that I remember thinking that no other life, however exciting or successful, could be as rewarding as the one I was living.

Those young men who were unable to keep up with the rigorous academic requirements were given a warning; if their performance did not improve by the next marking period, they were asked to leave the seminary.

Father Martin remembers that he spent many hours reading, studying, and contemplating in preparation for class discussions.

> Very often, during class, a concept would suddenly become clear and comprehensible as a result of something a professor would say, and at that moment all of the struggles with the text would become worth it. I remember how excited and invigorated I would be at those moments, and my admiration for the Sulpician professors grew even more.

During supper the seminarians listened to a homily presented by one of the deacons (a seminarian who was close to being ordained). Father Martin still recalls what an excruciating ordeal it was to deliver these sermons.

> Remember, the deacon was preaching to the entire community of 400 seminarians, and sitting right in front of him was what we called "murderers' row"—that is, the entire faculty. As the homily was being delivered, the superior and the other priests wrote down their critiques and passed them along to the rector. About once a month, the rector would read these critiques aloud to the entire community.

When people hear Father Martin speak about alcoholism, particularly when they hear him deliver the Chalk Talk, they marvel at the simplicity of his message. What they do not realize is that the "simplicity" of that message is the result of rigorous training in logic and reason and a profound understanding and love of humanity—acquired as a result of his years of study at St. Mary's Seminary.

By the time Father Martin completed his preparation for ordination, he had earned what is known as an STL, or Licentiate (license to teach) in theology. Far more important, however, he

31

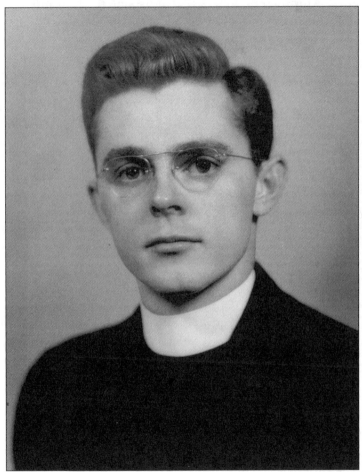

Father Joseph Martin on the day of his ordination. (Courtesy of Mrs. Dorothy Christopher.)

had developed an unshakable faith in God, an immutable devotion to the Catholic Church, and spiritual habits that would remain with him for the rest of his life. (Each day, Father recites the Divine Office, an official obligation of every priest, and the rosary; each morning he offers Mass and all his other prayers, works, joys, and sufferings to God; and each evening, in addition to the Act of Contrition, he recites this line from one of the hymns of Compline: "And what needs forgiveness dear Father, now forgive.")

As a result of his seminary training, Father's natural generosity and humanistic spirit were enhanced by a theological understanding of the interrelation between Christian doctrines and their practical application to Christian living—as St. Paul said, "Faith without good works is dead."

Joseph Charles Martin was 24 years old when he was ordained a priest on May 22, 1948, for the Archdiocese of Baltimore—a day he still describes as the happiest of his life. The day after his ordination, Father celebrated his first Mass at St. Mary's Roland Park with about 20 family members and friends present. Because Father Martin had been a member of the choir, Father Selner permitted him to choose the music to be sung, and Father still remembers his mother's reaction to the music.

> Father Leo Barley, who had married my parents (and for whom my brother Leo was named), had given my mother the leather-bound prayer book he read from during their wedding ceremony, and every time she attended Mass, she read from that book. But on the day of my first Mass, she said to me: "Joseph, the music was so beautiful, I couldn't concentrate on reading my prayers, so I closed the book and offered the music to God." It was an extraordinary moment for me, to realize the depth of my mother's spirituality—I was humbled by it and wondered if I would ever achieve such a simple holiness.

33

At the time of Father's ordination, it was customary for the mother of the priest to give her gold wedding band to her son so that it could be soldered into the neck of the chalice under the cup, and of course Marie Martin gave her wedding band to Joseph. Frances recalls what happened as a result:

> We thought it was terrible that our mother gave Joseph her wedding band; after all it was a symbol of her marriage. So the next day, she set off to buy another one. Remember, she was 52 years old at the time. She chose a ring that was identical to the one she had given to Joseph, and as she prepared to pay for it, the jeweler asked her if she would like to consider buying a ring for the prospective groom. Mother loved that story.

Although Father Martin celebrated his first Mass at St. Mary's Seminary, he sang his first Mass in his parish, St. Thomas Aquinas, the very next Sunday. The church was filled to capacity with Father Martin's former classmates, neighborhood friends, and parishioners who were proud that "one of their own" had been ordained. Father still remembers that "the greatest thrill of that day was seeing my father come to receive Communion from me. Just days before, he had gone to confession for the first time in 30 years."

After the Mass, Frances remembers standing next to her brother in the school hall, helping him to recall the names of the many people who waited in line to greet and congratulate him. As was the custom, people slipped envelopes into his hand containing money. There were refreshments, and Marie and James Martin beamed with pride and delight as they watched their son bask in the affection and admiration of so many people.

"Joseph had made so many sacrifices," Frances recalls, "he had studied so hard, and it was so good to see him enjoying himself. He was still very young, and he looked very handsome—that was a wonderful day, not only for him, but for the entire family."

Dorothy still remembers what Father Martin did with the money he received that day.

For years, Mother had washed and hung the laundry to dry in the basement, and because there was only a dirt floor there, she often came upstairs with her shoes covered in mud. This bothered Joe, and the day after the celebration at St. Thomas Aquinas, he gave the money to Mother and insisted that she have the floor cemented. It was so typical of Joe. Money just didn't mean that much to him unless he could use it to make someone happy.

Within two months of his ordination, Father Martin was given his first assignment: he would be sent to St. Joseph's College in Mountain View, California, a prep seminary serving the archdiocese of San Francisco, where he would teach "minor" seminarians—high school students preparing for the priesthood. It would be Father Martin's first time away from home, and Marie Martin was unhappy. By this time, Bernard, Edward, and Leo had left home, either to get married or to enter the service, and Frances had married a doctor named John Osborne, referred to by everyone as Jack (who would become one of Father Martin's best friends). Only Dorothy, who had just completed high school, and Marie remained at home. Marie, who had become a registered nurse, had just returned from England, where she had served valiantly during World War II. (One of her assignments had been to nurse the wounded coming back from the D-Day invasion at Normandy.) "California seemed very far away in 1948," Edward recalls.

My mother was taken by surprise when she heard that Joe was to go there. We could see how disappointed and sad she was. I don't think she ever said anything to Joe about it, but it was obvious to all of us that it was one of the most difficult things she had to endure. She talked about him all the time, wondering if he was in good health and spirits.

35

In addition to teaching seminarians, Father Martin assisted at St. Martin's Parish in Sunnyvale, California, on weekends. (Courtesy of Father Martin.)

Father Martin traveled by train to California in August of 1948 with another Sulpician priest, Father Bob Giguere, spending a day between trains at the Maryknoll House in Chicago. When Father Martin arrived in Oakland, he was met by two of the priests from the seminary who drove them to St. Joseph's, and he still remembers how "beautiful everything was, particularly the orchards that seemed to stretch for miles." St. Joseph's College in Mountain View had been founded by the Sulpicians in 1924, the year Father Martin was born, to serve students from more than 20 dioceses in the West. It was an extraordinarily beautiful seminary, nestled in the Santa Clara Valley near Palo Alto and San Jose, about 35 miles south of San Francisco.

Father Martin remembers that he "was given a few textbooks" in preparation for the classes he would be teaching in less than a month, and that the other priests who had been teaching for many years gave him advice and guidance. "I guess I didn't know enough to be nervous," Father recalls, "and I would be teaching my favorite subjects, English, History, and Religion, so I actually looked forward to the first day of class."

Not surprisingly, Father Martin was a success as a teacher. The students related to him immediately: He was young and funny, and he enjoyed their company. The stories, jokes, imitations, and anecdotes that had so pleased his contemporaries when he was a high school and college student, and later when he was a seminarian, had the same effect on his students. In addition, Father Martin loved language: he delighted in presenting puns and plays on words to the students, and he would often amuse (and instruct) his students by presenting word games and puzzles to them.

Father Gerald Brown (who would many years later become Father Martin's Provincial Superior) was a first-year student at St. Joseph's in Mountain View, and Father Martin was his Religion teacher. "I remember wondering what the seminary would be like," Father Brown recalls.

> I was away from home for the first time, and I was convinced that I would be living in a serious environment where everyone would be extremely pious. Having Joe as my teacher was so delightful: He helped the new students to see that a seminary could be a warm, human, even humorous place. His capacity to lighten things up while still being effective and maintaining the proper boundaries made him one of our favorite teachers. He was never too busy to talk with us; he'd come down to the playing fields in the afternoon to be with us.
>
> Once he took charge of the dramatics program, the seminarians really began to get interested in performing. He had a gentle way of drawing some of the quieter boys out and getting them involved. On the night of the production itself, Joe would be so excited it was contagious. I remember one particular performance when one

> of the seminarians managed to remember his
> lines; the entire audience heard Joe whisper from
> behind the curtain, "atta boy!"

In addition to being involved in the drama program at St. Joseph's, Father loved to sing High Mass and Benediction, and Father Brown remembers, "we noticed a difference immediately. Joe had a sweet, clear, fluid voice, and he clearly loved to praise God with music. The joy of his personality was very evident in his singing, as it was in all of his actions."

During Father Martin's first few weeks at St. Joseph's, he began a lifelong friendship with another Sulpician priest, Father Larry Taylor. Father Taylor taught Spanish, and on one of his trips to Mexico to study Spanish for the summer, he had become interested in bullfighting. His enthusiasm was contagious, and before long, Father Martin and he were reading everything they could get their hands on about bullfighting and bullfighters.

Father Taylor had fallen and injured his back several years before, and he was in constant pain. On some days, he would be unable to dress himself, and on those occasions, Father Martin would go to Father Taylor's room to help him get ready for class. Father Brown remembers, "Joe expected no recognition or credit for his kindness. He genuinely liked to help people. It gave him great pleasure and satisfaction."

Father John Olivier, who had been two years ahead of Father Martin at St. Mary's, was already teaching at St. Joseph's when Father Martin arrived, and he remembers that Father Martin was as popular and well liked at St. Joseph's as he had been in the seminary. "The students had nicknames for all of the priests," Father Olivier recalls, "and some of them were not so flattering. In fact, one of the priests, whose last name was Campbell, was nicknamed 'Beansey.' However, the students responded to Joe's youth, wit, exuberance—and bright red hair—by nicknaming him 'Pepper Martin.'"

On Thanksgiving Day, 1948, Father Martin, Father Taylor, Father Olivier, and another priest, Father John Thirlkel, decided to spend Thanksgiving Day together. It was an occasion that

Father Martin will never forget, because it was, he recalls, his "introduction to the martini." Father can recall the details of that day, "as if it happened yesterday."

> We were dressed in street clothes, and the four of us drove to a lovely old hotel in Santa Cruz for the afternoon. It was a holiday, we were away from home, and the four of us were happy to be in each other's company. I'd had a few beers in my life, but now I heard the other priests ordering mixed drinks; two of them ordered Manhattans, and Father Taylor ordered a double martini. Believe it or not, I didn't know what a martini was; I just pretended I did and said "I'll have a double martini, too."
>
> There are people who have to acquire a taste for gin, but I didn't—I loved it immediately. I had two or three doubles that day as we listened to the radio for two solid hours to some of the funniest comedians of the era. We didn't notice the time passing. I do remember feeling a wonderful glow and enjoying the day immensely. We returned and had dinner at Dinah's Shack near Palo Alto.

Father Martin continued to drink moderately for the next two years, always with others, and almost always at restaurants before dinner. "We usually had double martinis before dinner," he recalls. "There were many wonderful restaurants in the area. About every two or three weeks we could afford an evening out, drinks, dinner, and home, then up at 5:40 the next morning."

Apparently Father Martin's drinking had not yet affected his ability to conduct highly effective—and amusing—classes. Father Olivier remembers that Father Martin once explained to the students in his history class that the chariots used in warfare in ancient Rome had long, sharp daggers protruding from the wheels, "posing a great risk to the legs of the soldiers who got too close to them." After Father finished his explanation, he asked his students, with a perfectly straight face: "Do you know what the battle cry of these soldiers was?" When the students admitted they didn't know, Father broke into a huge smile, and imitating a battle cry, he declared: "Cut off my legs and call me Shorty." At lunch that day, the students in Father's history class told the other seminarians about the "Roman battle cry," and for months afterward, any seminarian could get a laugh simply by repeating "Shorty's battle cry."

Father Olivier also remembers that Father Martin would often mimic the older priests who had taught them at St. Mary's in Baltimore.

> Joe not only captured their voices, facial expressions, and mannerisms, he was so sharp and observant that he actually captured the substance of their thinking and personalities. These imitations were never cruel—they were conducted with great affection. Joe would always begin these imitations with the line, "Do you remember the way Father so and so used to...," and then he'd move into that priest's way of speaking and moving with such accuracy that the rest of us would shake our heads in admiration and wonder.

Father Martin's drinking began to increase, however, and his provincial, Father Lloyd P. McDonald, a gentle and sensitive man for whom Father had enormous respect, mentioned it during one of his visits to California. "I didn't lie about it when Father McDonald asked me about my drinking," Father Martin recalls.

> I had no fear of alcohol; I didn't think I had a problem, so I was perfectly honest. That may very well have been the last time, until eight years later, that I was honest about my drinking. In any event, Father McDonald said that he thought there was nothing wrong with an occasional drink, but I should be careful.

Father Martin was not careful; in fact, he began to drink every day. "I still didn't think there was anything wrong," he recalls, and I still wasn't drinking alone. Larry Taylor and I would have a few drinks in my room each evening after night prayers were over. We'd have long conversations about so many interesting things: spiritual matters, bullfighting, politics, the students' progress, teaching—we enjoyed the camaraderie—I never thought there was a problem, but I do remember becoming more conscious of making sure that I had enough in my room.

Father Martin had gotten into the habit of writing to his mother every week, but at about this time his correspondence became more erratic. Father remembers getting a letter from Edward,

in which he told me that one of the few things in life our mother had to look forward to was letters from me. I felt so ashamed of myself for being so careless, for not realizing how limited my mother's life had become now that her children were grown and on their own; I hadn't stopped to think about how much she must have missed having me closer to home. I never again let a week go by without writing to her.

Early in April of 1951, Marie Martin became suddenly and unexpectedly ill with uremia; her kidneys were failing. At that time, dialysis was not available. Father's sisters and brothers notified Father McDonald of the gravity of the situation, and he immediately arranged for Father Martin to fly home from California to be with her. Within hours of Father's arrival, Jack Osborne sent for an ambulance, and Father rode with his mother to Mercy Hospital, where he stayed with her for two days and nights. Marie Martin was in critical condition, and one of her last requests was that her son hear her last confession. "I still remember my mother asking God to be merciful to her, a sinner—it was so painful for me to hear her—this woman who had done nothing wrong, who had spent her life caring for others."

41

Marie Martin was only 65 years old, but she told Frances she did not mind dying because her three prayers to God had been granted: her children were grown and able to take care of themselves; she had seen her son, Joseph, ordained as a priest; and she did not owe anyone any money. The children were overwhelmed with respect and awe as they realized the simplicity and unselfishness of her requests. They were grief-stricken as well. Frances remembers that Joseph could barely speak; during the last two days of her life, he sat by her bed for hours, reading the Divine Office and praying for her—and for himself. "She may have had her wish to see her children grown," Father recalls, "but we weren't ready to live without her."

During the wake, hundreds of neighbors and friends came to pay their respects, and Frances remembers that there was some consternation when James Martin approached the casket speaking too loudly.

> He'd had too much to drink, of course, and we didn't want him to make a scene. They had been married for 38 years, and for most of those years my mother had put up with his drinking, so I guess none of us were surprised that he drank too much when she died. His grief was so deep that we almost couldn't blame him.

Marie Martin's funeral Mass was held at St. Thomas Aquinas, the church where she had been married, where her children had been baptized, and where her son had sung Mass a few days after his ordination. The church was crowded, not only with friends and relatives, but with priests who had come to pay homage to the woman who had been so generous and kind to them during their years at St. Mary's Seminary. Frances remembers that their presence was an enormous comfort to the Martin family, reminding them of their mother's goodness and generosity.

Father Martin returned to California soon after the funeral to resume his teaching duties and to cope as best he could with the greatest loss of his life. "I have always thanked God for one thing," he says, "that my mother was not aware of my drinking problem.

Father Martin, front row, second from right, and the seven priests with whom he completed the "Year of Solitude." (Courtesy of Father Martin.)

She would not have understood it; it would have hurt her deeply, especially since she had endured my father's drinking for so many years, and it would have caused her to worry about me."

In the fall of 1951, Father Martin returned to Baltimore to complete a Year of Solitude, a requirement for all priests who wished to become part of the Society of St. Sulpice. The purpose of the Year of Solitude (actually ten months) was to provide an opportunity for priests who had recently been ordained to continue their spiritual formation through prayer, spiritual exercises, and further study of the culture and history of the Sulpicians. The eight priests who participated had only three days off during the ten-month period: Thanksgiving, Christmas, and the Feast of the Annunciation. At all other times, the eight priests, along with a superior and an assistant superior, remained together in a separate wing, very often maintaining strict rules of silence.

Only upon successful completion of this rigorous period of study and spiritual contemplation could a priest place the letters "S.S." after his name: Society of St. Sulpice. Father Martin had admired the Sulpicians from the time he had begun to work at St. Mary's Seminary as a high school senior, and although the year was "the most difficult" of his life, he never doubted for a moment that he would be able to endure the strain imposed by the enforced solitude and inactivity. (The society has since modified the requirements to two summers rather than one extended period of isolation.)

In addition, Father did not drink during this period. "I remember the strain of the long hours of prayer and meditation," he recalls.

> I had grown accustomed to being with my students or with the other priests at St. Joseph's in California, always teaching or talking or preparing for classes, and now suddenly I was forced to spend most of my time alone, in contemplation. I couldn't have had a drink even if I wanted to; drinking was forbidden during this period. I don't think I craved alcohol, but I do remember thinking at the end of that period that I would be very happy to return to California.

Father Olivier had also returned to Baltimore at the same time to complete the Year of Solitude, and although he agrees with Father Martin that it was "the most difficult period of my priesthood," the occasional bright spots were a direct result of Father's personality.

> Joe was the center of our sanity simply because he was so upbeat and friendly. When we all griped about the difficult schedule we were forced to follow, Joe would let you know that he sympathized with you.
>
> Joe did his best to follow the rules and abide by the restrictions being imposed on us, but he did have one habit that got the rest of us in trouble from time to time. Those of us who were completing our Year were required to sit along both sides of a long, wooden table while the superior or an invited guest speaker sat at the head of the table giving a talk. It was hard to sit still and remain attentive; these priests would sometimes talk for almost an hour, and they would often repeat themselves or say something that we

thought was so old fashioned that we just wanted to scream. At these times, Joe would simply make a slight movement of his face; it was so subtle it couldn't even be called a grimace—just a twitch. However, his face was so expressive that he would send the men on the other side of the table into fits of laughter—for which they would be reprimanded of course—while Joe just sat there looking as innocent as could be.

Father Martin returned to California in 1952 and picked up where he had left off: with his teaching, with his friendships, and with his drinking. Father was still able to teach his afternoon classes with his usual enthusiasm—despite the hangovers—but he remembers that "the morning classes didn't go very well. How could they? I was usually too hung over to even remember what I was supposed to be teaching." Father Olivier remembers the changes in Father Martin's personality.

I never saw him drunk; I'm not sure any of us did. Instead, Joe just sort of disappeared. He spent all of his free hours in his room, away from the seminarians. When we did see him, he was quiet and preoccupied; the humor was gone; his eyes were flat; the Joe Martin who had made our world such a happy place was replaced by someone we barely recognized.

Father often describes incidents and events that occurred during his assignment in California in order to illustrate that, although his drinking was "unremarkable—your usual garden variety alcoholic," it was indicative of behavior that alcoholics often engage in: the belief that their actions are perfectly rational and reasonable. Father was convinced that he had devised a foolproof method for disposing of the empty bottles that continued to accumulate in his room. He'd wait until the afternoon bell for class had rung, indicating that all of the seminarians and professors were in their classrooms, then he'd walk out the back door

45

of the seminary, across a sloping meadow covered with beautiful green grass and wild flowers, toward the garbage dump about three quarters of a mile away, carrying two large suitcases full of empty bottles. "In my alcoholic thinking," Father Martin remembers,

> it never occurred to me that perhaps there was something odd about a priest, wearing a full-length cassock, walking toward a garbage dump in the middle of the afternoon carrying two suitcases filled with clanking bottles. Nor did it occur to me that every seminarian and priest who happened to look out the window of their classrooms would see me and wonder what kind of trip I was embarking on. What a sight I must have been.

"The drinking was easy," Father Martin now recalls ruefully, "getting rid of the empties was the hard part."

The next time Father McDonald visited California, he warned Father Martin yet again about his drinking, and this time Father Martin began to realize that "maybe there was something serious going on."

> Father McDonald told me that I had to realize that drinking and teaching seminarians just don't go together. Obviously, I agreed with him. I knew intellectually that having a couple of drinks just before hearing seminarians' confessions was a stupid idea; you've got to be a moron if you think they can't smell it, kneeling right beside you. But when you've had those two or three drinks, the thought means nothing to you.

Father Martin would occasionally help out at one of the parishes in San Francisco on Sunday mornings. "I remember one morning in particular. My hand was shaking so badly when I held the chalice after Communion that I had to steady it on the altar while the boy poured water into it. I had the shakes while I consecrated the Body of Christ—how much lower could a priest go?"

The next warning sign—one that Father couldn't ignore—was the hangovers. "I was drinking every day; I got into terrible shape and was put into the seminary infirmary. I began to think that I was heading for a nervous breakdown."

Father Gerald Brown, who had so admired Father Martin during his first year as a seminarian, was again assigned to one of Father Martin's classes during his fourth year.

> Father taught us Greek, and while he was still effective, the difference was noticeable. He wasn't as well prepared; he wasn't as alert; he wasn't as interested in talking with us and getting to know us.
>
> I also think that it was about this time that it was becoming more and more apparent to people that Father was drinking. I may have been aware of it sooner than some of the others because my father had been an alcoholic, so I was used to some of the signs—a lack of concentration, distraction, a loss of precision, a decline in inhibitions. He still told jokes and funny stories, but he didn't seem happy; that was probably the most telling sign of his growing problem.

Although Father Martin's superiors did not recognize that he was suffering from alcoholism, they became alarmed by his behavior, and in April of 1956, they placed him in the psychiatric ward of St. Mary's Hospital in San Francisco for "a complete rest." Father Martin was unable to function as a teacher, and he knew this, but he also knew that as long as he was away from the seminary, his colleagues would have to cover his classes for him, in addition to their own, depriving them of what little free time they had. "I was very unhappy and ashamed that I had let my students and fellow priests down, but I still didn't know what was wrong with me."

Neither did the doctors who treated Father Martin. Most doctors—like most laypersons—still viewed alcoholics as people who were too weak or too immoral to control their drinking, or as people who were drinking as a result of deep-seated problems.

No one even mentioned the word alcoholism during Father's three-week stay in the hospital; in fact, some friends who came to visit actually brought a bottle of wine as a get-well present.

Father did begin to feel better during his stay at the hospital, a result, probably, of his long walks in Golden Gate Park every afternoon. "Everyone wanted to know if I was happy," Father Martin recalls. "It was the classic behavior of people who do not realize that alcoholism is a disease—they think if they can find out *why* you are drinking, the drinking will stop."

In fact, the drinking did not stop. When Father Taylor went to pick Father Martin up from the hospital to drive him back to St. Joseph's seminary, the first thing they did was to go to a restaurant for dinner, preceded by their usual three double martinis. Father Martin still remembers the name of the restaurant, The Blue Fox, and he remembers as well that everyone had "the solution" for his drinking: get an outdoor hobby, keep busy, leave the priesthood.

Father's sisters and brothers became concerned when they heard that he had been admitted to a hospital in San Francisco, and they too had become aware that their brother was drinking too much, but they felt helpless and frustrated. "Joseph was so far away," Frances recalls, "and we were not being kept informed of the circumstances of his illness. It was almost as if we were no longer his real family, and we were reluctant to interfere."

In the late spring of 1956, within days of Father's release from the hospital, his superiors ordered him back to Baltimore, assigning Father's classes to three of the other priests at St. Joseph's. Father was informed that he was being given a new assignment: to teach the seminarians at St. Charles College in Catonsville, Maryland—the Sulpician's minor seminary.

It was not uncommon for priests to be re-assigned every few years, but it is quite possible that Father Martin's superiors thought that they could have more control over his drinking if he were nearer to the Provincial House. Father was assigned only two courses to teach during the 1956-57 academic year, another indication that his superiors sensed that he had a problem, one that was seriously affecting his ability to instruct and guide young seminarians.

Father Vincent Eaton remembers Father Martin's arrival at St. Joseph's Seminary.

> It was as if fresh air and sunshine had come into the building: his love of life and his ability to make people laugh was so refreshing and energiz- ing. Perhaps for that reason we didn't pay much attention to his drinking. When we would go out to dinner, Joe would often have too much to drink, but at that time there was nothing unto- ward or inappropriate about his behavior. That would come later. For the time being, it was just always good to have Joe around—that's the way everyone felt.

Hal Tulley, a lawyer who would many years later play a large part in the founding of Father Martin's Ashley, was a student in one of Father's English classes in 1956. There were rumors that Father Martin "had a problem with the bottle," Tulley recalls, "but his extraordinary personality and intelligence enabled him to function effectively." Tulley still remembers one of Father Martin's more dramatic entries into the classroom.

> Apparently, Father had developed a real interest in bullfighting, and he knew all of the motions that the matadors made. We had Father for our first class of the day, so it had to be very early, proba- bly about 8:00. Needless to say, none of us were wide awake. Suddenly, Father Martin swept into the classroom wearing his cassock and cape, took the long wooden pointer from the chalkboard ledge, and in one motion, rather deftly, threw his cape over the pointer, twirled around, and announced to the class that he had just performed a pass invented by Carlos Arruzza, a famous Mexican matador. Needless to say, very few of us knew what he was talking about, but he had cer-

tainly gotten our attention, and for the next 15 minutes he talked about bullfighting. From that moment on, he was our favorite professor.

Tulley remembers that whenever the students wanted to get Father Martin off the topic, they would simply start talking about bullfighting. "But Father was nobody's fool; he would only let us get away with that for a few minutes."

One of the most vivid memories Hal Tulley has of Father Martin as a teacher was Father's admiration for the work of Cardinal John Henry Newman, particularly his essays. "Father Martin was particularly fond of Newman's definition of a gentleman," Tulley recalls. "A gentleman is one who does not consciously cause pain. That was very important to Father; it seemed to be the way he wanted to live his life, and he thought it was as good a way as any for us to behave in our dealings with others."

Father Martin had always followed Newman's code—from the time he was a child making sure that the other children did not ridicule Ducky Neal because of his speech impediment. However, his alcoholism was impairing his ability to control his conscious actions: more and more, his thinking and behavior were clouded by the effects of alcohol. By 1957 Father's behavior was so erratic that his sisters and brothers stopped inviting him to their homes. "Joseph still told jokes and stories," Frances recalls, "but they began to be inappropriate, not funny, particularly in front of his young nieces and nephews."

Father Martin's sister, Dorothy, had married a man named Al Christopher, who had grown up in Hampden and had known the Martin children all of his life. Al and Father were good friends, but Father's drinking "certainly put a strain on our relationship," Al recalls. Father often received gifts from the parents of seminarians or for performing a baptism or wedding, and he began to use these gifts as excuses for getting his brother-in-law to come to St. Mary's at Paca Street, where he was living, to help him get rid of his empty bottles. "Our arrangement was very subtle," Al recalls.

50

We had an unspoken agreement between us. Father would say that he had this watch, and he didn't really like the way it fit, or he didn't really need it, and perhaps I could use it. Then he'd ask me if I could take some luggage out of his room for him. The luggage would be filled with empty bottles, of course, but neither of us ever said a word about it.

I remember, as if it were yesterday, that there would be as many as 40 bottles to get rid of. In hindsight, I can't believe that I did not confront him and make him come to terms with his problem, but we knew so little about alcoholism at that time. Now I realize that I was his biggest enabler.

Alcohol was sold in drug stores in Baltimore during the 1950s, and Father Martin (who still had not learned how to drive) would ask Al to take him to "pick up a few prescriptions," usually at the drug store on Wilkins Avenue. Al would wait in the car, and before he even saw Father Martin approach the vehicle, he would hear "the prescriptions" clanking against each other in the shopping bags.

Al and Dorothy's first child was born during this period, and of course they asked Father to christen their son. "I believe it was then that we all realized that Joe was being destroyed by his drinking," Al recalls.

It's hard to explain the change that had taken place in him. You've got to realize that he was a Martin, and all of the Martin children had always been known in our neighborhood and in our parish as intelligent, well brought up; the Martins were always proud and successful—earning scholarships, promotions, that sort of thing.

And of all the Martin children, Joe was the most special. He had always been popular and kind; he had always excelled in school—everyone knew about his scholarships. Then, when he was

51

ordained, it was as if he could do no wrong. It was as if he had fulfilled all of the promises that any parents could ever have for their children.

And now, although he was only 30 years old, it seemed as if he had destroyed that promise—we were literally watching him diminish—it was painful and ugly, and I suspect that we felt angry that he was doing that to himself—and to us. Little did we know that he had a disease; to us, Joe was a drunk. We didn't even use the term alcoholic in those days.

Frances still remembers the decline in her brother's appearance, and she remembers feeling relieved that her mother did not live to see her favorite son destroying himself.

Joseph was always so meticulous in his dress. Mother used to talk about his "handsome appearance." But he began to grow very careless about himself. I remember when he returned from California and we picked him up at the airport, he had stains on his clothing. I was shocked. It was so unlike Joseph; he was always so neat, well groomed, and handsome. I suppose we should have said something, but there was always that feeling that perhaps it was no longer our place. I do know that it would have broken Mother's heart to see him like that.

Father had developed a close relationship with Jack Osborne, Frances's husband. Because Osborne was a highly respected doctor, Father McDonald asked him to speak to Father Martin, knowing that if anyone could have an impact on him, it would be Jack Osborne. Father still remembers that conversation.

Jack was circumspect about it; he didn't want to embarrass me, but at the same time he realized that something had to be done. I remember telling him that although I wanted to stop drink-

ing, I couldn't. I was in agony; I knew that I was
not functioning in a priestly manner, but I didn't
know what to do about it. I had heard of
Alcoholics Anonymous, but it meant nothing to
me. I knew little about it; I just thought my
drinking was my problem and my fault, and that
I would have to pay the consequences.

When Jack asked me about my vocation, I
explained that it had never occurred to me to be
anything else. Again, it was that business of looking for the problem that was causing the drinking
rather than looking at the drinking as the problem.

Father Eaton, who along with the other priests had been so
delighted at Father Martin's arrival at St. Charles, recalls that by
this time, Father Martin's entire countenance had changed.

I don't think he told too many people, but his sister, Frances, had forbidden him to visit her home.
Joe was very upset about that. In addition, there
were only the faintest traces of his humor and
vitality; he was almost a shell. He always seemed
preoccupied, unable to concentrate. He grew
quiet and pensive, and I know that he no longer
conducted lively and interesting classes. He would
often give his students a reading assignment and
then just sit at his desk while they completed it.

By the end of 1957, Father had been drinking for almost ten
years, in increasing amounts, with increasing frequency, and with
increasingly disastrous results. He was no longer able to teach
effectively: his drinking had become more important than his
students, or just about anything else for that matter. Father
remembers those two and a half years teaching at St. Charles as
"the most horrible period of my life." He can still describe the
pattern that he began to follow: he would go to his room as soon
as he could; there, he would drink shots of vodka from the bottle he kept in his bathroom, not caring about his students, his

work, or himself. "However, I was not in denial," Father Martin recalls.

> I knew exactly what I was doing, and I knew that everything that was wrong in my life could be traced to my drinking. I just didn't know what to do about it. I remember one night in particular, locked in my room, absolutely alone, standing in the corner like a caged animal. I had returned the bottle of vodka to the shelf in the bathroom knowing that I'd already had too much and that I would suffer in the morning, but I went back to that bottle for four more shots. I had lost all self-control, along with my self-respect.

Father Martin remembers the compassion and patience that his provincial, Father McDonald, exhibited throughout this period.

> Every time Father McDonald came to St. Charles, he sent for me. Of course, I dreaded those visits because I was scared to death of what I was doing to myself and what would happen to me. During one of those meetings, Father McDonald said to me, "What do you want? If it is humanly possible for me to give you what you want in order to stop you from drinking, it's yours." I just stared at him; what could one say in the face of such kindness?
>
> On another occasion, Father McDonald had me admitted to a hospital in Baltimore, just to keep me from drinking during the holidays. I remember sitting alone in a hospital room on Christmas Day 1957 thinking about my family and how I was not with them; thinking about my fellow priests and how I was not with them; and thinking about my students and how I had failed them. If there were ever motivation for me to

stop drinking, that was it, and because I did not stop drinking, I felt even more unworthy.

Alcoholics have many bad days—certainly more bad days than good—as the disease progresses and begins to adversely affect relationships with family, friends, employers, and, of course, themselves. However, Father Martin's agony was compounded by the fact that his behavior and actions were so antithetical to the life he had fervently hoped to lead as a priest, the life for which he had studied and trained for five years. Ministering to the spiritual needs of others and to the educational needs of future priests suddenly seemed more and more an impossibility: Father Martin was beginning to fear that he was unable to even save himself. Never was he more aware of this than on the day he lied to his provincial.

> Of course, Father McDonald was losing patience with me; who could blame him? Finally, he sent for me and after a very brief and terse hello, he said: "Joe, I want no more lying. Have you been drinking?" I said "No, Father." Of course I knew very well that he wasn't asking if I had been drinking at that moment. I knew I was lying by interpreting the question for my own convenience; Father McDonald knew I was lying, and I knew that he knew. Yet, I could not tell the truth. I was too afraid and too ashamed. It was the most self-degrading thing I had ever done—to lie to someone who wanted to help me and who knew the truth.
>
> What I wouldn't have given to stop drinking forever at that moment—but I just sat there staring at Father McDonald, and I noticed that he had tears in his eyes. I was causing my Provincial such great pain.

There was one further humiliation. A few weeks after the conversation described above, Father McDonald informed Father Martin that his services assisting at Our Lady of Victory parish in

Baltimore, where he said Mass on Sundays, would no longer be needed: the pastor had received too many complaints from the parishioners about his drinking.

Father Martin was being crushed by his disease—and he did not know what to do about it.

> The last few months of my drinking, I was afraid to go near the altar during the week. I would go down for morning prayers and meditation, but then I would go right back up to my room. I would lie on my bed, stare at the ceiling, and shake in fear—I didn't know what I was afraid of—everything I guess. I knew that God did not hate me, but I believed that He had just quit in complete disgust. I felt that if I died at that moment my soul would be put into some celestial orbit—alone. That's how I felt. Not lonely—alone—absolutely alone.

In June of 1958, almost ten years from the time that Father had drunk his first double martini, Father McDonald went to see him; it was a meeting that Father Martin will never forget because it changed his life forever.

> As Father McDonald walked in I said to myself, "he's probably going to send me to some out-of-the-way seminary where I'll just be kept hidden, where I won't cause embarrassment." I would have no contact with students, no classes to teach; I would be making no contributions to the Sulpicians. I was 34 years old, and the priests who had educated me now had to find a place to hide me so I wouldn't cause scandal and embarrassment.
>
> Instead, Father McDonald said to me: "Son, we are sending you away this summer. This is not punitive; we just want you to get well." Although he was sending me away—it wasn't to a place

56

where I would be left to die—it was to a place that had helped other priests, a place in Michigan called Guest House. Suddenly, a great wave of relief came over me. I thought, finally someone is doing something—because although I had tried and tried, I couldn't do anything to help myself. I cried that evening—not in mortification or fear—but in relief.

Father Martin packed some clothes, and Father McDonald drove him to stay with Frances and Jack Osborne for a few days before he made the trip to a place he had never heard of and knew nothing about: Guest House in Lake Orion, Michigan, not far from Detroit. It would have been too risky to leave Father Martin alone in the seminary now that classes were over and the seminarians had gone home for vacation. Although the feeling of relief remained with Father Martin, feelings of guilt and shame returned: his family had always looked to him as the most successful of all the Martins; now they had to take him in because, in effect, there was no place else for him to go. "The shame I felt that day, June 15, 1958," Father recalls, "cannot be described. I felt like a failure before my family, before the Sulpicians, before myself, and before God."

Father's feelings of guilt and worthlessness were exacerbated by the fact that June 15 fell on a Sunday—the first Sunday of his life that he ever missed Mass. "I was so low that I would have had to jump up to touch bottom," he recalls.

Father Martin said goodbye to his family ("We didn't have much to say to each other," Frances recalls), boarded a plane for Detroit, and was met at the airport by a fellow Sulpician, Father Lyman Fenn. Father Martin still remembers "how kind and gentle he was at that terrible time in my life." Father Fenn drove him the 75 miles to Guest House, where he was welcomed by the director, Austin Ripley, who introduced himself, Father recalls, "with great sincerity and warmth."

Meeting Austin Ripley was probably one of the most fortuitous events of Father Martin's life, and, given the fact that

Father Martin's lifelong devotion to helping alcoholics recover was a direct result of his experiences at Guest House, one of the most fortuitous events ever to occur in the world of alcoholism recovery.

CHAPTER THREE

Good Things Will Happen in Your Life

Within five minutes of meeting Austin Ripley, Father Martin decided, "I want to be just like this man." He still recalls their first meeting:

> I find it difficult to define charisma, because there are so many different kinds of it, but I sure know it when I'm near it. If Austin Ripley had said to me, "I want you to sleep on the floor your first month here," I would have done it and not asked him why. Somehow I just knew that he knew what to do. Within the next few minutes, Rip explained to me what was wrong with me, and I was convinced utterly, once and for all, that I am an alcoholic. Then, he spoke the most encouraging words I've ever heard, telling me that I was sick, very sick, but not evil.
>
> Next he gave me the best piece of advice I've ever had in my life, and I pass it on to anyone with this problem: I know all about your education, your degrees, your background. He said, "Father, your brains didn't work, did they?" Having had my last drink just the evening before, I had to say "no." And so he gave me this advice: "Leave your brains right outside the door. You do not need brains to get well, you need desire." Whatever it was inside this man's soul that he had, I wanted. And I knew

when our brief interview was over that he knew
and understood me.

It is not surprising that Austin Ripley (whom everyone called
Rip) knew and understood Father Martin—particularly the suffering, humiliation, and despair that Father had endured as an
alcoholic. Not only was Ripley a recovering alcoholic, he was a
devout Catholic who, by the time Father Martin met him, had
devoted 15 years of his life to the recovery of alcoholic priests
(that is the way he spent the rest of his life as well). Austin Ripley
knew and understood the special circumstances alcoholic priests
endured: When their drinking became known, they were subject
to more criticism than the layperson, because priests are held to
far higher standards in our society. Furthermore, when priests
sought refuge and recovery in A.A. meetings, other recovering
alcoholics often did not just see someone with a problem but
someone to whom they could tell their troubles and bare their
souls.

Ripley also knew of the type of "treatment" these priests had
often received: transfers to out-of-the-way locations where their
drunkenness wouldn't cause too much scandal; admission to hospitals where they could "dry out" with no treatment whatsoever
for their alcoholism; and, as a last resort, admission to psychiatric
institutions where they were "treated" for the "problems" that
were presumably causing their drinking.

In fact, it was for those reasons that Ripley had started Guest
House two years before: to create a private sanctuary where
Catholic priests could begin their recovery by learning about the
Twelve Steps set forth by Alcoholics Anonymous without embarrassment, without the needs of others interfering with their
recovery, and in the care of those who understood the special circumstances that exist for alcoholic priests.

The very fact that Ripley had succeeded in creating Guest
House is a testimony to his brilliance, devotion, and tenacity: At
the time, most of the people in authority in the Catholic Church
(like most laypeople) did not know that alcoholism was a disease;
they perceived it as a character flaw, as a sign of weakness or

moral turpitude. Furthermore, very rarely did the Church approve of, much less support, the interference of outsiders in dealing with the problems experienced by religious.

A lifelong friendship began between Father Martin and Austin Ripley on the very day that they met—a friendship that they both valued—but the friendship between these two outgoing, intelligent, funny, and charismatic men was not the primary reason for Father Martin's recovery. Rather, it was the philosophy of Guest House itself, where the dignity and worth of every individual who came there to recover from the disease of alcoholism was recognized and respected. In fact, more than 20 years later, when Father (inspired by a most extraordinary woman, Mae Abraham) established his own treatment center, he modeled it on Guest House because it was there, for the first time, that he "was treated by people who understood my disease and who treated me with dignity and love."

At Guest House, a large, stately tudor mansion located on 53 acres of beautiful lawns and trees, Father, along with the 15 other priests who were in residence at the time, was assured of the three elements that Austin Ripley believed were essential to the recovery of priests: an adequate length of stay, support for their religious vocations, and the presence of other clergy to help them realize they were not alone in their problem. Ripley did not simply admire the work that priests did, he believed that priests were "a tremendous gift of God to the Catholic Church." He had established Guest House for one reason: to aid those who served his God and his Church. In fact, the preamble to the Philosophy of Guest House, a document prepared by Ripley to explain the purpose and function of Guest House, reads:

> Because in His ministry, Christ, Our Lord, placed such emphasis on healing the sick—the sick in body, mind, and soul—we who are privileged to found Guest House, and we who serve here, would imitate Him in this respect.
>
> To this end we, the members of Guest House, bind ourselves to the acceptance of His ideals as

guides in the establishment and conduct of Guest House; and all who succeed us, in whatever capacity, likewise are bound. Let no one serve at Guest House in any capacity, who has not deep pity for the sick alcoholic priest and religious, great hope for their recovery, and respect for their high faith in the healing power of God.

The preamble is followed by a description of the guiding principles set forth by Austin Ripley; it is a document that does nothing less than guarantee that the dignity and worth of every visitor be protected—and enhanced:

> Each guest-patient shall be treated as priceless in the eyes of God;
>
> Guests at this house shall not be regarded as penitents;
>
> Charity shall be dispensed with open handed delicacy so that the sensibilities of guests shall never be offended;
>
> No one at Guest House shall counsel another in sobriety, or in anything else, unless it be done in humility and love;
>
> Everyone serving at Guest House shall be guided by our Lord's command to St. Catherine of Siena: "You should all have compassion on each other and leave judgment to Me";
>
> We at Guest House shall serve humbly. Arrogance and pride must be foreign to all who enter this high service;
>
> However menial the job, or remote the contact with guests, all who serve here shall be motivated by the desire to help those who would recover from their sickness;
>
> Whatever the guise that is worn, the guests who enter this House for treatment will be sorrowful. It is our privilege to comfort them wisely and treat them effectively so that they

may return to the world joyful in their high vocation.

In addition to establishing an environment that Father Martin remembers as "one of the safest, most serene, and most secure places I have ever been in," Ripley used his own experiences as an alcoholic to model for the priests who came to Guest House what Father Martin describes as "the essence of the Twelve Step Program, one alcoholic saying to another, 'let me tell you what happened to me.' That is what sells sobriety, the example of others who have gone before you—hearing their story and realizing that if they recovered, you could too."

Austin Ripley told his story to every priest who visited Guest House, and it was an extraordinary one. His father had been a college professor but decided that sending him to college would be a waste of time. Rather, he educated his son by inviting colleagues over for dinner two or three times a week; in that way, Austin could learn from their conversations rather than in a classroom. Apparently, this plan succeeded: By the time Austin Ripley was 12 years old, he was serving as a page boy in Congress. As a young adult during the 1930s, Ripley devised a system to teach illiterates to read and write that was adopted by the Armed Forces. He was soon hired to train other teachers in his method—and despite the fact that he was often inebriated—he managed, through his system and through his training program, to help thousands of men who had joined the Army during the Depression learn to read and write.

By the mid 1930s, Ripley began to write what would become one of the most popular crime series in this country. Called "One Minute Mysteries," he presented "crimes" that could be solved in one minute if the reader paid careful and close attention to the clues given in the single-column text. These mysteries were published daily in the *Chicago Tribune* and weekly in *Look* Magazine, where they were called "The Photo Crime Quiz," because the description of each crime was accompanied by a photograph containing clues. Ripley's editors and publishers knew that he was rarely sober, but as long as he produced his copy on time no one cared. His first marriage had failed as a result of his drinking, and he had little contact with his two children. His drinking placed an enormous strain on his second marriage as well.

Ripley would give up drinking every Lent, but on Easter Sunday he'd begin where he had left off. It was those periods of abstinence that actually fueled his alcoholism, because he used them to rationalize that he could stop drinking whenever he wanted. In fact, he once promised his mother, on his knees and in tears, that he would stop drinking for a full year, and he kept his promise. When the year was over, however, he began to drink again, and because alcoholism is a disease that progresses regardless of whether one is drinking, he began to drink far more heavily and with far more dire consequences at the end of that year of abstinence. His health was beginning to be affected, of course; on one occasion, he almost died of pneumonia. Furthermore, he alienated and antagonized everyone for whom he wrote at both the newspaper and *Look* Magazine—he may have been a brilliant writer, but he was a very nasty drunk.

One evening, during the period when Ripley was living in Washington, D.C., he found himself in a hotel room, alone and inebriated. He had bought a copy of *The Saturday Evening Post,* and it contained an article about Alcoholics Anonymous. The article described the success of the five-year-old organization, and it described the "big book" that had been published only one year before. It was one of the first articles ever written about the fledgling organization, and Ripley was fascinated by it. As a result, he picked up the phone, got the number of the local A.A. organization from the operator, and dialed it. Within an hour, there was a knock at his door.

By that time, Ripley had reconsidered his actions. Leaving the chain on the door, he peered through the crack at the two men and one woman standing there and asked them to leave, telling them there had been some mistake—he certainly had not made the phone call. They would not be deterred however. One of the men spotted a bottle on Ripley's night table and said, "Aren't you at least going to invite us in for a drink?" With that, Ripley released the chain.

Not only did they *not* have a drink with Ripley, they brought him to a hospital. One of the men, Charles Sullivan, stayed with Ripley day and night, although Ripley informed him that he intended to get drunk the minute he was released, and in fact, that is precisely what he did.

"Give up on me," he told Sullivan. "I'll die this way, I know." When he returned to the hospital, so did Sullivan, and when Ripley finally asked him what he wanted, Sullivan replied: "I want to see you sober."

It was a turning point in Ripley's life. For years family, friends, and employers had been saying the same thing to him, but this time the words of a stranger keeping vigil at his bedside made all the difference—Austin Ripley stopped drinking—and he remained sober for the rest of his life.

Soon after his release from the hospital, Ripley left Washington and returned home to Colfax Island in Wisconsin, where he and his second wife, Lee, owned a winterized cabin. Once there, Ripley couldn't forget Charles Sullivan, particularly the things Sullivan had told him about A.A. Ripley did not drive, so he asked his wife to drive him to Eau Claire where there was a weekly Saturday night A.A. meeting, the only one in the area. When they arrived, they discovered that the meeting was being held in a small room above a bar. When Ripley entered, he found four older men talking about their drinking experiences and why and how they had stopped. Ripley sat politely for about 20 minutes and then, losing patience, he asked when the A.A. meeting would start. One of the men looked at him and said, "Start? You've been in it for 20 minutes!" Ripley was incredulous—this couldn't be the great movement he'd read about in *The Saturday Evening Post* and about which Charles Sullivan had spoken for hours on end. But as Ripley listened—and talked—he began to understand the genius of A.A. He would later describe it to the priests at Guest House as "the greatest university on earth—where priest learns from plumber how to live."

Ripley was so impressed by the logic and effectiveness of A.A. that for the next year he spent as much time as possible with the founders of Alcoholics Anonymous, Bill Wilson and Dr. Bob Smith, in order to discover as much as he could about these two men and the organization they had founded. (Father Martin is convinced that Rip had as much influence on these two extraordinary men as they had on him.) By the end of that year, Ripley had become one of the leading proponents of Alcoholics Anonymous in the United States. In fact, he may have unintentionally begun one of the earliest Al-Anon meetings: while he and the other recovering alcoholics had their meetings, he would arrange for the spouses and children of the A.A. members to boat out to his island cabin, where they would swim, picnic, and, of course, talk about their experiences.

Austin Ripley abandoned his writing career and devoted himself to Alcoholics Anonymous, attending meetings, speaking, and starting groups. However, he began to notice that although the Twelve Steps had a tremendous impact on the lives of so many men and women, the priests whom he took to the meetings very rarely attended regularly enough or long enough to benefit—and almost all of them relapsed again and again. Ripley would often take a special interest in these priests, offering to be their sponsor, contacting them, helping them in any way he could, but nothing he did seemed to help.

Ripley began to sense that alcoholism had a somewhat different effect on priests than it did on laypeople: He noticed that the shame and self-hatred felt by priests seemed to be deeper, more intractable. Priests, Ripley noticed, often felt that either they had betrayed God or God had betrayed them. And despite this emotional and spiritual turmoil, lay members attending the A.A. meetings still expected recovering priests to minister to their needs—they did not see only a fellow struggling alcoholic, they saw a priest. And in some cases, particularly in small communities, that priest may very well have been their confessor. (Ripley had written to Bill Wilson about some of the "problems of the alcoholic priest as being different from those of the layman," and

66

Wilson had agreed with him, responding, "That their case has special, even unique aspects, is not even debatable.")

By the early 1950s, Austin Ripley had decided that he would try to help alcoholic clergy by establishing a facility for the exclusive use of Catholic priests. He obtained an option to buy a piece of land in Minnesota and began discussions with some business people in that area about opening a treatment center for Catholic priests. These people thought that the facility should be used not only for priests, but for other professionals as well. Ripley finally withdrew from that project, still determined to open a facility for the exclusive use of alcoholic priests. (The project in Minnesota did go forward—and it resulted in the opening of Hazelden—one of the most famous recovery facilities in the world.)

In 1949 Ripley delivered a lecture entitled "The Guest House Concept" at a conference held in Rensselaer, New York, in which he tried to win approval for his idea by explaining "the truth concerning the problems of the alcoholic priest." Ripley criticized the Church for its handling of the problem, claiming, "In the Church's attempts at reform of the alcoholic clergy, we see the grim and dreadful tradition of the past, and the fearful, frightful acts of the present." The Church, Ripley explained,

> often engaged in a punitive psychology—one of punishment, penance, and discipline.... Punishment for a disease! Because of this the Church continues to sow the shocking mistakes of the past and it continues to reap an unholy harvest of sickness, shame, and scandal. The awful price of its folly is wrecked lives, abandoned vocations, and despair.
>
> When will the Church recognize and have the humility to admit that past methods have failed tragically? When will it be admitted that the alcoholic priest is a sick man, however gross a sinner he may also be, and that if intelligence does not prompt it, charity demands that it be treated as

such? And when will proper treatment and reha-
bilitative facilities be provided?

Ripley further alienated Church authorities by arguing that a
treatment facility for alcoholic priests not only could be run by
a layperson—it *had* to be run by a layperson in order to ensure
the priests the two conditions essential to recovery: a place where
they were no longer under the authority of a superior who probably knew little or nothing about alcoholism and a guarantee of
absolute confidentiality.

Ripley admitted that "the hierarchy, provincials, and superiors
of the Church have a sympathetic and charitable attitude toward
the alcoholic priest in the beginning of his illness," but when
misguided attempts to solve the problem fail, the superior, "confronted with an alcoholic priest who does not respond to initial,
kindly treatment, with the serious obligation to prevent scandal,
acts finally in frustration...." (Ripley was describing the same situation that would confront Father Martin nine years later: on the
day that Father Martin sat in his room waiting for his provincial
to arrive, he felt the same fear that thousands of priests before
him had felt, that he would be sent as far away as possible to prevent scandal.)

Ripley was finally able to open a small facility in Chippewa
Falls, Wisconsin, in 1951, but within a year of its opening, the
local bishop violated the contract that he and Ripley had signed.
Ripley lost control of the guest house he had worked so hard to
establish, but he took his case all the way to the Vatican Court and
won. As a result Pope Pius XII gave Austin Ripley his official
blessing to start a facility for Catholic priests. (There is no other
case in recent history of a layperson defeating a bishop in a
Roman court of Canon Law.) Given the attitude about alcoholism that existed among laypeople and particularly among
members of the hierarchy of the Catholic Church, the fact that
Ripley won both the case and the Pope's approval was absolutely extraordinary—a testimony to his tenacity and courage (and
the beginning of a recognition among Church officials that alcoholism is in fact a disease).

Austin Ripley next set his sights on the magnificent Scripps Estate in Lake Orion, Michigan. The tudor house, designed by its wealthy and prominent owner, Edward Wyllis Scripps, the founder of United Press International, was modeled after several European manor houses and castles. It was large enough to accommodate 16 priests, but the real reason Ripley was so determined to buy the estate was because it contained a large high-ceilinged room with magnificent stained-glass windows. Even before Austin Ripley met Mrs. Scripps, the owner of the house, he decided that he would use that room as the chapel. Mrs. Scripps was not interested in selling the estate, but Ripley kept visiting her, explaining his mission, begging her to sell the estate to him, until she finally relented.

The response of church officials to Ripley's plan to open a facility for priests in Michigan was overwhelmingly positive; in fact, it was Cardinal Edward Mooney of Detroit who furnished Ripley with the $70,000 down payment for the estate and who arranged for the remainder of the money to be provided through a low-interest loan. (Cardinal Mooney told Ripley that the down payment had been donated by "three businessmen who wished to remain anonymous," but Ripley always suspected that the Cardinal had used his own funds.) Ripley never forgot Cardinal Mooney's generosity, and whenever he spoke about Guest House, he thanked the Cardinal and several other bishops and priests for their "considerable vision and genuine courage."

Guest House officially opened in June of 1956. During the first two years of its operation, the staff would often go without pay so that other, more pressing expenses could be met. The patients never suspected that there were financial difficulties, however. Austin Ripley believed that the greater the illness, the better the treatment and facilities should be, and so he did everything in his power to ensure that the priests were, quite literally, treated as honored guests at his house. ("Guest House should not be concerned with the cost of treatment," Ripley had once said in describing his vision, "it should be concerned exclusively with providing the best possible treatment, regardless of cost. Do not

69

Austin Ripley at Guest House. (Courtesy of Mr. Richard Koehn.)

the lives and souls of the ordained of God transcend all dollar evaluation? What price a priestly life?")

By the time Father Martin arrived in June of 1958, Guest House had begun to earn a reputation among Church superiors and provincials as the place where priests had the greatest chance of getting well. In fact, Austin Ripley was beginning to earn respect—and financial support—from some of the very same bishops who had initially opposed him. (Although Ripley was never able to abandon the time-consuming process of fund-raising, Guest House was never again as strapped for funds as it had been during its first two years of operation.)

Dick Koehn, who worked with Austin Ripley at Guest House for more than 27 years, remembers that Ripley sometimes worked 20 hours a day in order to keep Guest House running: Fund raising took enormous time and energy; maintaining correspondence with the superiors of the priests who were in residence also required an enormous amount of time—and diplomacy; and Ripley was also responsible for overseeing the hiring and training of staff. Then, after everyone else had gone to bed, Koehn remembers, Ripley would read the latest books, articles, or studies about alcoholism, and incorporate the material into his lectures.

Despite such a grueling schedule, Ripley never let a day go by without showing affection and concern for every priest who entered Guest House. When Father Martin once asked him, "How far do you go to help an alcoholic?" Ripley replied, without hesitation, "As far as you can, and then one step more."

Ripley often told the priests that one of the first things to return with sobriety is a sense of humor, and Father's sense of humor not only returned, he used it to bring pleasure to the other priests. Priests who were in residence at Guest House at the same time as Father remember that if they heard a burst of laughter coming from a certain room or area, they knew that Joe Martin must be nearby.

Ripley believed that the priests at Guest House should feel that they were in a place where dignity and decorum would

always be maintained. Therefore, although the priests were free to
dress casually in order to hike, fish, and boat during the day, they
were asked to wear clerical garb for meals, the rosary (recited
together in the chapel before dinner), and at meetings. Ripley
always wore a suit. In fact, few people at Guest House ever saw
him in shirt sleeves. (It was a practice that so impressed Father
that he would enforce a staff dress code at his own treatment center 25 years later.)

Father Martin still remembers attending his first A.A. meeting
the night after he arrived at Guest House. "I had heard of
Alcoholics Anonymous," Father recalls,

> but little did I know of its power to heal. I re-
> member thinking, "this is so simple." Through
> Alcoholics Anonymous, I slowly began to realize
> what was wrong with me—as amazing as this
> sounds. And I began immediately to feel an enor-
> mous sense of relief: finally, I knew what was the
> matter with me, and I was beginning to learn—as
> early as the first meeting—what I could do about it.
>
> I think it was the simplicity of Rip's definition
> of alcoholism that helped me to come to terms
> with the fact that I was an alcoholic. "If you can
> connect your drinking—either before, during, or
> after—to any major problem in your life, then
> you've got a drinking problem. And the name for
> that problem is alcoholism."

Father recognized and valued Ripley's expertise: "He knew
what was available to know, and a little more," Father has said.
However, another aspect of Ripley's behavior left an even deeper impression on Father Martin: the humility and honesty with
which he approached the Eighth Step, to make a list of the per-
sons whom he had harmed while he was drinking and attempt
to make amends to every one of them.

In Ripley's case, this was not an easy thing to do: He had alienated or ostracized practically every executive at *Look* Magazine.
Determined to make amends to the best of his ability, Ripley

flew to New York, took a cab to Manhattan where the magazine's executive offices were located, took an elevator to the top floor, and began to work his way down, apologizing one floor at a time. He intended to start at the top with the chief executive officer and end with the doorman. Austin Ripley was as well known for his arrogance as he was for his brilliance, so many of the executives to whom he offered an apology were shocked at his humility and sincerity. Ripley explained the precise purpose of his mission, explaining that his sorrow was as sincere as his intention to follow the Twelve Steps to recovery.

There was one executive, however, who refused to be moved by Ripley's request for forgiveness. He did not offer Ripley a seat, and before Ripley could even finish apologizing, the man said: "Get the hell out of my office. You were an arrogant son of a bitch when you were drunk, and you're an arrogant son of a bitch now. Who do you think you're kidding?" Ripley could feel the anger and humiliation rising in him, and he stormed out of the office and waited for the elevator, determined to take a cab to the airport and go back home. While waiting, however, Ripley thought, "Have you forgotten the forgiveness you've already been given? And have you forgotten that there are people to whom you still owe an apology?" Referring to the man who had humiliated him, Rip said: "He didn't have to accept my apology, but I had to give it." When the elevator arrived, he went to the next floor and continued to seek forgiveness.

Some of the priests would express their fears to Austin Ripley that although others might accept their apologies, how could they come to terms with the way they had offended God. "God is forgiveness," Ripley would reply. "You're just not that good at being that bad. There is nothing you can do that is bigger than God can forgive." Ripley would conclude almost every lecture by promising his guests that although there was little else in life that he was sure of, he was sure of this one thing: "If you stay sober one day at a time, good things will happen in your life."

Father Martin remained at Guest House for seven months, with the full support of his provincial, Father McDonald. Priests

Dr. Walter Green at Guest House.
(Courtesy of Bruce and Robert Green.)

were not forced to leave Guest House after a certain preordained period of time; they left when, and only when, Ripley felt they were ready to leave. Along with meetings, lectures, exercise, good food, and an opportunity to re-establish a relationship with God (an opportunity that was greatly·enhanced by the Guest House chapel and the five altars set up to ensure that every priest could say Mass each morning), the priests were given a series of lectures by Dr. Walter Green who, like Austin Ripley, had first-hand knowledge of the disease.

Dr. Green had been one of the most prominent physicians in Michigan; in fact, he had been the director of Brighton Hospital in Brighton, Michigan. However, his uncontrolled drinking eventually affected both his professional and personal life. Although he was still able to practice medicine, his wife had divorced him, and as a result, for several years, he saw very little of his three sons. After Dr. Green recovered through A.A., as an act of gratitude for his own recovery, he devoted the rest of his life to the care and treatment of alcoholics. ("You don't get A.A.," Green was fond of saying, "it gets you.") Austin Ripley often said that no one in the United States possessed the knowledge of alcoholism that Dr. Green, whom he always referred to affectionately as "the little

Doc," possessed, a knowledge matched in size and degree by his humility, honesty, and charity. Dr. Green never accepted payment for the hours he devoted to the priests at Guest House. Father Martin has described him as "one of the most remarkable human beings I have ever had the pleasure of knowing."

Although Father soon became immersed in the history of Alcoholics Anonymous and developed a deep and lasting respect for Bill Wilson and Dr. Bob Smith, he was particularly struck by the logic of Dr. Green's lectures—probably a result of his own training in philosophy and theology. "Doc Green had a positive genius for simplicity," Father recalls, "and a brilliant awareness of the importance of stating the obvious."

Father recognized immediately the similarity between Dr. Green's discussion of the intellect and the emotion and St. Thomas Aquinas's observation that man is a rational animal: first he thinks, then he judges, then he acts on that judgment. Father began to take notes during these lectures, particularly when Dr. Green discussed the way that drugs caused the emotions to over-rule the intellect. "I can't think of a better description of a normal man than this," Dr. Green told Father Martin and the other priests who had gathered to listen to him:

> He is a man in whom the intellect rules over the emotions. When a man's brain is drugged by alcohol, he begins to follow his emotions rather than his reason. And since alcoholism is a progressive disease that grows inevitably worse—never better—we find in the course of time a complete reversal of normal behavior, and the emotions rule.
>
> There have been many different agencies trying to do something for the alcoholic. And of course, we know what they are. The first one we come in contact with, naturally, is our relatives, our family. Although we don't recognize that we have retreated or reverted to childish behavior, they recognize the childishness and treat us as a child with reproach. We call it nagging. They are

nagging us to death. Friends sympathize; doctors are indifferent; psychiatrists are in despair; sociologists treat the alcoholic with scorn. Nobody has treated the alcoholic with understanding.

It is difficult to understand that a simple drug, ethanol, ethyl alcohol, can completely reverse a man's life. [Alcoholism] starts with a low tolerance for drinking that increases gradually, and then it drops—two drinks now do what it used to take a fifth of a gallon to do. Along this path we begin to develop those childish characteristics, the characteristics of the alcoholic. And my friend, even my identical twin, can partake of this drug, even as I could at one time, with impunity. But for the alcoholic, somewhere along the line, something has happened. We are all familiar with allergies; something happens. We don't know what it is... And we begin this descent into oblivion.

Father saved those notes—cherished them in fact—and 14 years later, he would use to them to prepare a talk on alcoholism that would eventually be heard by hundreds of thousands of people in the United States and around the world.

In December of 1958, Father Martin received word that Frances's husband, Jack Osborne, had died of a heart attack. Father was disconsolate: Jack had been one of his best and most loyal friends throughout his struggle with alcohol, never condemning or berating, always offering friendship and help. Furthermore, Osborne was only 42 when he died, at the height of his powers as a highly respected physician in Baltimore. His death reminded Father of his own mortality, and, on a more practical level, left Frances alone with three very young children.

Father was permitted to leave Guest House in order to conduct the funeral Mass and help console his sister, but he then returned to Guest House for one more month. Father "did not even think of having a drink" during his trip to Baltimore. All of the conditions for a relapse existed, of course, but Father Martin had learned his lesson well: "You must be clean and sober before you can resolve any other problems," Austin Ripley had told him again and again, and he was indeed sober as he helped his family get through their loss.

During the last three months of his stay at Guest House, Father Martin assisted at a parish in Oxford, Michigan, hearing confessions on Saturdays and saying Mass on Sundays. For the first time in many years, Father Martin was performing his priestly duties sober. He told Ripley, "Guest House is the most priestly house I've ever been in. I wish I could stay here forever." Ripley just smiled and said, "No Father, you don't really want to stay here. When you are ready to go home, you'll want to. You'll want to get on with your life."

Ripley was right, of course. By January of 1959, Father was ready to go home, but Guest House had become an integral part of his life: he would return for visits and retreats whenever he could; he would maintain a correspondence with Rip until Ripley's death 15 years later; he would contribute as much money as he could afford to Guest House; and in every lecture he delivered, he credited Austin Ripley and Dr. Walter Green with teaching him everything he knew about alcoholism.

It is impossible to describe accurately and completely the effect that Austin Ripley, Dr. Walter Green, Guest House, and the Twelve Step Program had on Father. He says they changed his life forever, and while this is of course true, it does not begin to explain the transformation he underwent during this period of his life. Father often talks about the way his stay at Guest House helped him to understand, for the first time in his life, the true meaning of freedom. Rollo May, the renowned humanist psychologist, has said that true freedom can be achieved only when a person has developed the ability to consciously choose how he or she will respond to the external demands of the environment. Clearly, Guest House, Austin Ripley, and Dr. Walter Green had made Father Martin a free man. Father often tries to explain the permanent and profound impact that his stay at Guest House had on him by citing something he learned from Austin Ripley:

Rip told us that Bill Wilson was once asked what he meant by "a spiritual awakening." Bill said that it couldn't be defined as easily as it could be recognized: look for a profound change in personality. Rip would tell us that sobriety would bring back the man or woman who existed before alcohol or drugs injured his or her life, along with something greater—and that something greater is a result of the suffering, because God uses pain as the fertilizer for spiritual growth.

That is as good a definition as any to describe Father Martin's transformation during his seven-month stay at Guest House—an already good man made even greater as a result of his suffering. Father Martin left Guest House determined to live the Twelve Steps, and in so doing, he was eventually able to bring the peace and joy of sobriety to thousands of people and their families.

This successful transformation did not occur immediately however. Everyone who participates in the Twelve Step Program knows that healing takes time, that happiness and productivity do not return overnight. In fact, the longer one drinks, the longer it usually takes for one to recover fully in body, mind, and spirit. Father Martin never drank again after he left Guest House, and he thanked God every day for the freedom and joy of sobriety.

However, changes were beginning to occur in the Church, and in society, that would have a permanent and profound impact on Father Martin: the need for full-time teachers of seminarians had begun to decrease, and he would not begin to use his extraordinary talents as a teacher in the field of alcoholism on a full-time basis for several years. Father would encounter many problems during the ensuing years, and he would endure loneliness and frustration, but he never forgot what he had learned at Guest House: one must be clean and sober in order to resolve any other problems. As Austin Ripley had said over and over, "If your sobriety does not come first, there will be nothing to come second."

CHAPTER FOUR

❦

Trust God, Clean House, Help Others

*F*ather Martin returned to Baltimore in January of 1959 filled with confidence and enthusiasm. He had learned much about his disease—and about himself—during his seven-month stay at Guest House, and in addition to becoming active in his local group (he attended his first meeting less than a week after he arrived home), he felt ready to resume his duties teaching the young seminarians at St. Charles. Father's first assignment upon his return was to teach high-school-level courses in Religion, History, and English.

A letter Father Martin received from Austin Ripley dated February 17, 1959, could only have bolstered his confidence: "We have never had a guest," his good friend wrote, "nor do we expect to have one, who has or will do a more honest, sincere, and total-ly magnificent job of recovery and self rehabilitation than you. Hence your past is discharged, your present secure, and your future assured, even with such a distraction as your Afghanistanian wolf hound, Val!" (Father Martin had acquired a dog and named it Prince Valiant; it was actually a German shep-herd.)

The affection that Austin Ripley felt for Father Martin was apparent in one of the last paragraphs of that same letter:

> All of us here miss you, Padre mio. And everyone who knows you sends you his very warmest good wishes. No mere conventionalism this…they mean it. You endeared yourself to all of us. Just

These notes, taken by Father Martin during Dr. Green's lecture, became the basis for the Chalk Talk. (Courtesy of Father Martin.)

know that you are frequently in my thoughts, daily in my prayers, and always in my heart. And I am unspeakably grateful to you, Father Joe, for your great charity in remembering me each day at Holy Mass. What magnificent payment this is for the privilege that God gave me of playing a role, however small, in your wondrous rediscovery of self.

Ripley closed his letter by agreeing with something Father Martin had said about the efficacy of the Twelve Step Program: "You know, we know, that it always works, when you work it."

Father Martin began to attend three or four meetings a week, following Ripley's advice to "go to more rather than less." Shortly after Father returned to St. Charles, he asked a friend to teach him how to drive so that he could get to meetings. Father recalls it was at these meetings that he began to deliver what became known as his "Blackboard Talk":

> When I came back from treatment, I joined a group called Ten Hills on Edmondson Avenue in Baltimore. As a member of that group, when your turn came, you chaired two meetings: On one Thursday night, it was a discussion meeting, and on the next Thursday night, it was a speaker's meeting at which someone would deliver a talk.
>
> I didn't know that many people in Baltimore who could be a speaker for me, so I decided to use the notes I had taken from Doc Green's lectures to give a simple presentation myself. I still had the piece of paper with the notes written on both sides, and they happened to have a blackboard at the meeting place. It seemed like a natural thing to do: I'd make notes on the board and comment on them, then I'd make a few more notes and do the same thing. This had not been rehearsed.

There were a few members from other groups present, and they asked me if I would give my "Blackboard Talk" to their groups as well. I carried that piece of paper with me from meeting to meeting, until I had the talk memorized and didn't need it anymore. Believe it or not, that's how the Blackboard Talk started.

In 1959, Father Martin returned for a visit to Guest House and spoke to the priests who were in recovery at the time. When Father arrived home, he found a letter from Ripley waiting for him, thanking him for "his magnificent contribution."

You will not know, Padre mio, the joy in my heart at hearing you talk to the priests at the House meeting. That was as fine, as directly on-the-target A.A. talk I have ever heard. Heavily freighted as it was with perfect sincerity it reached the heart—even of the newly arrived and still skeptical. Don't ever, ever, lose your enthusiasm! This tired and jaded world affects a sophisticated tiredness, a flippant philosophical condescension, toward enthusiasm. Dead in emotions, mind and soul, the unenthusiastic yet retain the ability to realize their own poverty and hence trigger their envy of the enthusiast with the dead hand and cold fingers of faint and weary opposition.

What a truly magnificent contribution to life and to God lies before you. Indeed what a wondrous thing God has wrought in your life. He is now preparing you for great things.

Although the primary purpose of Ripley's letter was to thank Father for his talk to the priests, Ripley's references to the "unenthusiastic" and their impact on the "enthusiast" were probably intended to help Father Martin deal with the response he occasionally received from people who did not understand Alcoholics Anonymous. There were people who thought it unseemly that a priest would talk about his alcoholism in front of groups of peo-

Father Martin during one of his visits to Guest House. Over the door is a legend that reads, "None Come Too Soon, None Leave Too Late." (Courtesy of Father Martin.)

ple, wearing a Roman collar. Old attitudes die hard: having a drinking problem is bad enough, but talking about it all the time was even worse. Even Frances, Father's sister, expressed shock when Father invited her to attend a meeting at which he was the featured speaker. "You're not going to tell them about your drinking problem, are you?" Frances remembers asking her brother. She quickly changed her mind, however, when she heard her brother address the crowd of 200 people. "He was so logical and compassionate," she recalls, "that he got a standing ovation. I was very proud of him, and I learned more about alcoholism in that one evening than I had in my entire life."

Father Martin was gratified by Frances's response, of course (since the death of his mother, he had grown very close to his older sister), but he was not looking for approval. He knew that carrying the message to other alcoholics was as important to his continuing recovery as it was to theirs—he had only to look at the experience of Bill Wilson and Dr. Bob Smith, the co-founders of Alcoholics Anonymous, to know that. Furthermore, his training as a priest had helped him to understand why he gained so much pleasure in talking about his recovery to others. "Goodness is a gift from God," Father Martin explains. "And goodness, by its very nature, must be shared."

In 1961, two years after Father's recovery, Austin Ripley invited him to attend a meeting that was to be held for recovering alcoholic clergy in New York City. Bill Wilson lived in the area, in Bedford, New York, and Ripley asked him to address the priests. It was the first and only time Father Martin heard Bill Wilson speak, and he has never forgotten the occasion.

> He was strikingly handsome with a tall, slim, military bearing. He told his story and answered questions, and I knew I was at the feet of the master. My only regret was that I only had about two years of sobriety at that time; I wish I'd had 20 so that I could have more fully understood the wonder and magic of the moment. I understood of course what A.A. had done for me, but I didn't fully appreciate the influence that the organization was having on thousands and thousands of people. That would come much later as I traveled around the country, and then around the world, seeing the way the Twelve Step Program literally saved and transformed lives.

It did not take Father long to realize that despite his recovery and his desire to resume his teaching duties, changes that were taking place in the Sulpician Society, in the Church, and in the country itself would have an enormous impact on his future. At about this time, a meeting was held among the Sulpicians to discuss the problems that existed with the traditional curriculum being offered to the seminarians and to discuss changes that could be implemented. One of the results of these meetings was the decision to stop using the texts of Adolphe Tanquerey, the very texts that had been the basis of Father Martin's theological training. They would be replaced by a more open-ended approach to dogma, one that was not so rigidly defined. In effect, although Father was only 35 years old, his seminary training was considered part of the "old order" rather than the new.

Then, in 1962, Pope John XXIII opened the first session of the Second Vatican Council. Although he died less than a year later, his successor, Pope Paul VI, conducted three more sessions, and during the next four years, reforms were implemented in the Church that would force Father Martin—and many other priests—to make changes and adjustments in their attitudes, their performance, and their commitment to a Church that had, seemingly overnight, changed radically and inexorably from the one they had known all their lives.

The changes engendered by the Second Vatican Council were followed by a precipitous drop in vocations in the United States, resulting in fewer young men entering seminaries. The decline was being caused by several trends that were occurring simultaneously in the United States: the civil rights movement, the feminist movement, campus unrest, anti-war protests, and the liberalization and reform of the Church. In the mid 1950s, the Sulpician seminaries across the United States had been teeming with seminarians; by the mid 1960s many seminaries were being consolidated—and some closed. Not only were there far fewer new vocations, many priests and sisters were leaving their societies or orders.

At about this time, it was decided that St. Mary's Seminary on Paca Street would no longer be used to house seminarians. Most of the property was eventually purchased by the city and turned into a park. Only the Mother Seton House and the chapel remain. The feeling of loss among the Sulpicians who had lived there was severe: the sense of order, of continuity, and of tradition that the priests had come to know and love was gone forever.

Amidst these changes—some would even say chaos—Father Martin recalls that he "just wanted to get on with my priesthood." But it would not be that simple. When Father first returned to Baltimore, and for the next several years, he was given a relatively light teaching load, but he was as popular with the seminarians at St. Charles as he had been at St. Joseph's. In

1959 Father directed a production of *My Three Angels* (after the performance, the cast and stagehands brought him out on stage where he received a standing ovation); in 1960 Father directed a production of *Mr. Roberts;* in 1961 he directed an adaptation of *Arsenic and Old Lace;* and in 1962, *A Bell for Adano* according to the seminary's newsletter, "was a stellar success," thanks to Father Martin's "deft hand." In 1963 the newsletter claimed that under Father Martin's direction, *Me 'n' Ben* was also a success—"almost professional." By 1963, however, as vocations began to decrease, Father Martin's teaching duties were reduced to three courses, then to two, until by 1966, he was teaching just one course a semester to a dwindling number of students.

Father did not object. Nothing was more important to him than his sobriety. "No matter what I was asked to do," he recalls,

> it would not have mattered. I wouldn't have cared if they asked me to look for moles in the yard. Father McDonald, my provincial, had arranged for me to go to Guest House where I met Austin Ripley, the man who saved my life. I had been brought back from the pit of hell, and I had begun to realize that God had bestowed upon me the greatest blessing in the world: sobriety. They say your worst day sober is infinitely better than your best day drunk, and I've never forgotten that. The shame, the lying, the physical discomfort, the emotional turmoil, the spiritual degradation were gone. I thanked God every day for this blessing.
>
> Austin Ripley used to say, quoting Doctor Bob, that the Twelve Steps could be described in six words: "Trust God, Clean House, Help Others." And that's precisely what I set out each day to do—knowing that if I succeeded, the rest would fall into place. And I remembered as well something else that Rip would often say to us: "There are some alcoholics who don't see an enormous

86

improvement in their lives after three or four months, and they grow discouraged." Rip would pause for a moment and then say, "How many years were you drinking? How many years did it take you to get in the condition that brought you here? Do you think you're going to see a dramatic change overnight? Of course not. In recovery, time is of the essence."

Furthermore, although Father did not realize it at the time, a new passion had begun to develop in him, one that would, in fact, become his primary focus in life. Still a great teacher, and still able to captivate an audience, Father Martin continued to talk about alcoholism wherever and whenever he was asked. The people who heard him speak knew that they were in the presence of an extraordinary communicator, much as Father Martin had felt when he first heard Austin Ripley. By the mid 1960s, although Father perceived his talks as nothing more than behavior that was essential to maintaining sobriety (Step Twelve), his reputation as a compelling and effective speaker had already begun to spread among groups in the Baltimore, Washington, and Philadelphia areas.

In 1968 Father Martin was informed that he would no longer be assigned teaching duties; instead, his primary responsibility would be to serve as Chaplain for the Oblate Sisters of Providence at their convent and mother house in nearby Catonsville, Maryland. These sisters, members of the first black religious community in the United States, had been closely associated with the Sulpicians from the time their order was founded in 1829, and a Sulpician priest had always served as their chaplain.

The assignment consisted primarily of saying Mass each day and having benediction for the sisters—duties that took no more than two hours—a perfect assignment for an older priest. In fact, it was an assignment that was usually filled by members of the Sulpician order who had become too old or infirm to continue their teaching duties. Father Martin, however, was only 44 years old.

Of course, Father realized that although his education and training had prepared him well to teach high-school-level courses, he did not possess the training or the advanced degrees required to teach graduate courses. As the minor seminaries staffed by the Sulpicians across the country continued to close, it was those Sulpicians who had completed advanced degrees who were assigned the theology and philosophy courses still being taught in the major seminaries.

Father Martin continued to speak at meetings, usually in the evenings, and every morning he drove to the convent to celebrate Mass for the 200 nuns in residence there. The sisters looked forward to Father's arrival—he usually had a funny story to tell, and he was dedicated to the sisters' needs. "It was an honor to be their Chaplain," Father recalls. "These women were doing God's work with a rarely found spirit of happiness and dedication." In addition, Father had begun to assist the pastor at St. William parish in Baltimore on Sundays. "That's the way I supported myself," Father recalls.

> I would receive a stipend for helping at the parish
> and one from the convent, and I didn't need very
> much money. I did begin to feel at this point that
> I was certainly not as active or involved as I would
> have liked. But there was nothing I could do
> about it. There was a certain feeling of regret; I
> wouldn't call it depression, but I was beginning to
> feel outside of things, and I had a lot of time on
> my hands.

In addition to this feeling of isolation, Father Martin underwent surgery first for a hiatal hernia and several months later for bi-inguinal hernias. Although it took several weeks after each surgery for him to regain his strength, Father put the experience of being placed under anesthesia to good use. Dr. Green had described to Father Martin and the other priests at Guest House the effects of alcohol on a human being, comparing it to the effects that ether had on a patient in a lecture entitled "A

Comparison of Ether and Alcohol." Now, Father could speak from personal experience when he described the similarities.

But the two operations, combined with the fact that Father often found himself with little to do for days at a time, contributed to a growing feeling of malaise. Although Father maintained contact with his sisters and brothers, and although he was once again a welcome guest in their homes, they had their own careers and families.

In 1969 James Martin died in a nursing home. He was 83 years old, but in old age he had not changed very much—he was still uncommunicative, displaying little emotion or affection for his children. In fact, Frances still remembers an incident that occurred while she kept vigil at her father's bed the day before he died:

> I was 55 years old, married, and with a family of my own. Dad asked me if my children were in school. I replied "yes." He turned his head toward me wearing the same stern look he had always worn. "Yes, what?" he said. "Yes, sir," I replied. Even on his death bed, he was making demands on his children, utterly unaware of the sacrifice I was making to be there for him.

Although James Martin's death did not have the same effect on Father as the death of his mother, it left him with a lingering sense of melancholy. "I used to visit him in the nursing home," Father recalls,

> and I'd see him lying there, with no interests, few friends, no enjoyment, no reason to live. He had never really overcome his drinking problem, and after he retired, he had no purpose in life—my mother had held our family together, and after her death, he was particularly lost.
>
> I guess I started to wonder if my life would end in the same way. I didn't talk about this with anyone at the time; I'm not even sure I articulated

89

these concerns to myself, but they were there, in
the back of my mind. I felt my life was without
purpose, and my own inability to generate an
interest or a project made matters worse. I had too
much time on my hands. People kept telling me
how valuable my Blackboard Talk on alcohol was,
and I certainly didn't need recognition to be
happy, but I did wonder if I had anything to contribute; I wondered if I was leading a useful life.

Father Martin blamed himself for his inactivity, claiming that
although he had earned degrees in philosophy and theology he
should have been awarded an honorary degree in laziness.
However, the situation he found himself in by the late 1960s was
not entirely of his own making. Throughout his adolescence and
early adulthood, Father Martin had devoted himself to studying
and training for the priesthood. Particularly during the years at
St. Mary's, there had been little time to develop hobbies or interests. The seminarians were being trained to serve God and His
Church; for five years, every moment of their day was filled with
study and prayer.

Then, less than two months after ordination, Father had been
sent to California to teach high-school students. There was certainly no way he could know that within ten years, teaching posi-
tions at this level would be eliminated. For ten years, his alcoholism had robbed him of any opportunity to develop interests
that could later be used to occupy his spare time. Although he
loved to read, particularly literature, he soon discovered that "you
can't read for seven hours a day." Father Martin's exercise routine
was limited to occasional walks. Father continued to give his
Blackboard Talk, but it was all he had.

Father did maintain contact with Austin Ripley and Guest
House, however, looking forward in particular to Ripley's letters.
Although he was earning very little money at the time, every
Christmas Father sent a gift to Austin Ripley—so that "other
priests could benefit from Guest House as I had."

In 1967 Father Lloyd McDonald, the provincial who had been so kind to Father Martin and who had arranged for his stay at Guest House, resigned because of a serious illness, and Father Paul Purta replaced him. Father Purta's provincialate has been described in official Sulpician publications as the "embodiment of the new spirit of modern stewardship," but there didn't seem to be a place for Father Martin in this new environment. Early in 1969 Father was transferred from St. Charles back to St. Mary's at Paca Street, where the former seminary was now being used as a retirement home; Father Martin was no longer teaching, and he would be living with about eight or nine priests who were much older than he.

As the new provincial set about determining the needs and goals of the Sulpician priests he had recently been elected to lead, one can just imagine him wondering what to make of—and what to do with—this recovered alcoholic priest. Furthermore, the Sulpicians had to confront the financial and administrative realities that had resulted from the decline in vocations: they simply could not continue to support those priests who were no longer teaching.

Father Martin was informed by his new provincial that a decision had been made at a meeting of the Sulpician Provincial Council that in order for the Society to adapt to the "reality of the times," those priests who were not actively involved in the "special mission" of educating seminarians would be "invited to resign" their membership in the Society of St. Sulpice and function instead as diocesan priests. Father accepted the "invitation"; in actuality, he had little choice in the matter. He wrote to Austin Ripley telling him of his transfer to St. Mary's on Paca Street and of the spiritual and emotional agony he was enduring. He had been using the letters "S.S." after his name for more than 20 years; now he was being released from the very institution that had formed him. Austin Ripley sent Father Martin his "love and prayers" in a letter dated July 7, 1969, along with "the hope that you survive the hazards of Paca Street."

Father Martin did survive these hazards, but it was a very close call. His behavior began to grow more erratic: He was unable to sleep or concentrate; he was calling family, friends, and acquaintances in the middle of the night, unaware of the time; and not even the extraordinarily positive response his Blackboard Talks continued to receive could alleviate his feelings of worthlessness. Father had met a young man named Stuart Bramble at one of the local group meetings, and they had become good friends. Every evening, Father would call Stu and keep him on the phone for hours. "I knew he had just gotten home from work," Father recalls, "and that he had other things to do. But I needed to hear a friendly voice; I needed something to keep the loneliness and feelings of desperation and depression away. Stu had the patience of a saint—he had the kind of giving that asks no rewards. But I tested that patience every night for months."

By 1970 Father was so despondent that he was relying more and more heavily on the tranquilizers a doctor had prescribed to help him sleep. He continued in this state for several months, "often not knowing day from night," until, fearing for his sanity—and his life—he placed one more late-night phone call, to a woman who had heard one of the Blackboard Talks he had delivered more than five years earlier at Johns Hopkins University. In 1959 Austin Ripley had saved Father Martin's life. Now, his life would again be saved by a recovered alcoholic—Mae Abraham.

No one could have predicted the effect the friendship that developed between Mae Abraham and Father Joseph Martin would have not only on Father Martin himself, but on the field of alcoholism. No one could have guessed that these two people, so different in background and temperament—one a Catholic priest from Baltimore, the other the daughter of a Baptist minister from the mountains of North Carolina—would have even become friends.

Mae Abraham's given name was Lora Mae Ashley—and she was called Lora Mae throughout her childhood. The fifth of 11 children, she was born on July 24, 1927, on a farm her family had owned for generations in West Jefferson, North Carolina, near the Tennessee border. Although Mae's parents were not well educated or wealthy, the family was highly respected because of her father's ministry. Reverend Arthur Ashley provided for the spiritual and temporal needs of the members of his congregation quietly and steadily, with little fanfare or need for recognition, and it was this quality, above all others, that endeared him to the people in the community.

Mae remembers that her life was no different from that of the other people in her community:

> Our lives were hard, particularly my mother's, because of the enormous responsibility and burden of bearing and raising 11 children. She was only 15 when she got married, and the children were never more than two years apart. Her whole life was spent caring for us. But she didn't seem to mind, and because all the families in the community were large, supporting themselves mainly through farming, none of us felt deprived or neglected. We didn't know we were poor, and we were certainly loved. Although there was affection and warmth, we were taught to respect and obey our elders, particularly by my father.
>
> Our lives consisted of helping with the farm chores, going to school, and going to church. We would attend services that would last for hours; the hymns were wonderful but the sermons were very long.
>
> We were surrounded by acres and acres of beautiful farmland, and there was always an abundance of food from our own crops, so we were self-sustaining; we took pride in the fact that we could provide for ourselves and not have to rely on others. We learned early in life the value of work.

93

Among the many other lessons the Ashley children learned from their parents, especially their father, were the evils of alcohol. "We were taught that anyone who drank would go straight to hell; it was that simple," Mae recalls. "Those who drank were weak-willed, with no self-control or self-respect, bent on destroying themselves and their families." Mae was also inculcated, from an early age, with the belief that all Catholics, and Catholic priests in particular, should not be trusted. "All of the superstitions of a small and isolated rural community came to bear on my beliefs about Catholics," Mae recalls. "We were told as children that Catholics had horns and tails. And we believed what we were told."

Although Mae loved and admired her parents, the person who probably had the greatest influence on her was her grandmother, Cora Williams (actually her mother's stepmother), who lived with the Ashley family throughout Mae's childhood.

> My grandmother's husband died the month before I was born, so I filled a void for her. She loved all of the children, but there was something very special between us. I went wherever she went; I did whatever she did. We all lived in the same house, but she had separate quarters, and for as long as I can remember, my bed was always in that section of the house, next to hers.

Although Mae's grandmother (whom she called "Maw") never received formal medical training, she functioned as a practical nurse, and she was known and respected throughout the community for her knowledge, compassion, and ability to help those who were sick or disabled. Mae's grandmother (whom everyone else called Aunt Cora) took Mae with her whenever she made a sick call. "She was very special," Mae recalls. "She ministered to people with patience and skill. They loved and admired her. I always tried to help in little ways, and she encouraged me. There wasn't anything she wouldn't do to help someone get better or feel more comfortable."

Mae at age 5 with her grandmother, Cora Williams. (Courtesy of Mrs. Mae Abraham.)

Mae's life was sheltered, and her activities were closely monitored by her parents. "We did not date in those days," she recalls. "We went to school, came home, did our chores and homework, talked and prayed in the evening, and went to bed. Girls who did differently soon earned a bad reputation, and my parents made certain that we stayed home where we belonged." In fact, Mae was not permitted to attend her high school senior prom because her father did not approve of dancing.

Mae loved school and was a good student, earning straight As throughout high school. Although it was relatively rare for women to attend college in that time and place, Mae was determined to continue her education, and her parents supported her decision, permitting her to attend a business college in nearby Elizabethton, Tennessee. Shortly before the semester began, Mae arranged to serve as a caretaker for a 90-year-old woman in return for room, board, and spending money. In that way, she could reduce her parents' financial burden and, in addition, her parents were assured that she was "in a proper home."

Mae still remembers it was at college that she encountered young women who actually had more clothes to wear at school than she had owned in her entire life. "For the first time," Mae recalls, "although I had always known there were people who had much more money than my family did, I started to understand that the word 'poor' could accurately be used to describe my family's circumstances." Mae cared for the woman with whom she lived with the same gentleness and patience that she had seen her grandmother exhibit. "That woman was very lonely," Mae recalls. "Mostly, she just wanted someone to talk to. I was able to do my homework assignments while listening to her tell stories about the Civil War. She had actually witnessed several battles—she had some good stories to tell."

At the end of her first year of college, Mae decided to join her sister, Mary, who had moved to Aberdeen, Maryland, for the summer, where she would work as a waitress. Mae hoped that she would be able to save enough money to cover her second-year tuition, thus relieving her parents of an enormous financial burden. The United States had entered World War II at about this time, and Aberdeen was teeming with soldiers.

It was in Aberdeen that Lora Mae's name was shortened to Mae, and within days of her arrival, three soldiers began to come into the restaurant every evening and sit in Mae's station. One of the soldiers, Tommy Abraham, had noticed Mae, and his friends agreed to accompany him to the restaurant to "lend moral support." Tommy remembers that he "fell for Mae immediately." One could hardly blame him. She was very beautiful: her auburn hair, fair skin, and sparking blue eyes, coupled with her soft southern accent and her shy, modest demeanor, were absolutely irresistible. Mae refused Tommy's initial requests for a date but relented when he would not give up.

Mae was also attracted to Tommy; he was unlike any man she had ever known. Tommy had been born and raised in a small town near Pittsburgh, and he seemed sophisticated to Mae, even worldly. Mae celebrated her nineteenth birthday with Tommy in July of 1946; two months later they were married, having known each other for less than a year.

Mae's parents were disappointed; they had hoped that she would be the first Ashley to graduate from college. Furthermore, they sensed that Mae was not ready for marriage and that she did not fully understand what she was getting into: Tommy loved to have fun, and that often involved drinking, smoking, gambling, and partying late into the night—activities that were perfectly ordinary and acceptable for soldiers—but activities that were not entirely appropriate for the husband of a young woman who had not been on a date before she met him. Mae assured her parents that they had nothing to worry about; all Tommy needed was a good wife to settle down.

Tommy was discharged in 1947, and he and Mae moved to Pittsburgh to be near his family. Mae was unhappy; she was in a northern city, away from her family, and she soon discovered that Tommy's "war-time" behavior was carrying over into peace time as well. Matters were made worse as Mae began to realize that in Tommy's family it was accepted that a man was entitled to have fun while his wife waited at home.

Mae's sister, Mary, sensing Mae's growing unhappiness, urged her to return to Aberdeen to resume working at the restaurant. Mae agreed, concluding that the only way her marriage could possibly succeed would be if Tommy joined her in Aberdeen, where they could have a fresh start. Tommy did join Mae, and he was soon able to find a job. However, both Tommy and Mae were coming to the realization that although they loved each other very much and wanted the marriage to succeed, they were so different in background, in temperament, in religion (Tommy was Russian Orthodox), and in their attitudes about what constituted proper behavior that they would have to struggle constantly to make their marriage work.

Mae was further troubled by the behavior of her two older sisters, Mary and Grace, and one of her brothers, Carl. They had begun to drink so heavily that their marriages and careers were being affected. Moreover, their drinking was causing Mae's parents great sorrow and shame. "Remember, we did not view alcoholism as a disease," Mae recalls, we viewed it as a terrible weakness. I remember being furious at my sisters and brother for causing my parents such sorrow and shame. I could not understand how they could seemingly ignore everything our father had told us throughout our childhood about the evils of drinking. I could only conclude that they had some perverse reason for wanting to hurt my parents—and themselves.

I had never had a drink in my life and believed I never would. I was terribly ashamed of my brother and sisters. I used to moralize to them about their behavior; I was convinced that they could stop drinking if only they could be made to understand that it was evil and bad. I must have been insufferable.

Mae had always promised herself that she would never drink; however, as her relationship with Tommy continued to worsen, she began to rationalize that it was her behavior that was causing the problem. Perhaps Tommy would be more willing to spend evenings with her if she were not so prim and proper. One night, Tommy suggested a Tom Collins, describing it as "a summer drink, like lemonade, but made with gin." It would be "refreshing," he assured her.

Mae had three drinks that evening, and she will never forget the consequences: She developed fever blisters and was unable to keep even sips of water down, much less food. It took Mae two weeks to recover fully from what was a serious allergic reaction to alcohol. "I thought I had learned my lesson for good," Mae recalls.

I vowed never to drink again. I thought God was punishing me because I had always promised Him that I would never drink. And I kept my promise for two years. But I was still unhappy with Tommy's behavior, and I was feeling terrible emotional and mental turmoil. I simply assumed that the problems we were having were my fault, and finally I decided that I would go out with Tommy and have a good time, and of course a good time included alcohol.

I became as ill the second time I drank as I had the first time, but I could not stop drinking no matter how sick I became. There were occasions when the alcohol would make me so sick I would have to be taken to the hospital, but I simply could not stop drinking. I went to doctors who told me that I was suffering from "nerves"; one doctor put me in the hospital for what he called "a good rest."

Tommy and I were still very unhappy, and a miscarriage that occurred about three years after we were married only made matters worse. I visited marriage counselors, clergymen, psychiatrists, doctors, and as incredible as this sounds, no one identified my alcoholism. In fact, one doctor encouraged me to have a drink before meals to help me relax and to increase my appetite since I had lost so much weight.

When I became pregnant with Alex, both Tommy and I thought that a child would be the solution to our marital problems, but when he was born in 1956 matters became even worse. I was drinking uncontrollably and was still getting violently ill; Tommy had begun a restaurant business and he was spending more and more time out of the house either at the restaurant or with his friends.

We fought constantly about my drinking: I would promise Tommy that I wouldn't drink, but I could never keep my promise. I would blame my drinking on his behavior; he would say that my drinking caused his behavior. We were locked in a vicious cycle, and our little son, Alex, was paying enormous consequences. No child should have to endure what he experienced during the first eight years of his life.

Tommy finally decided to have his mother come and live with us so that she could look after the baby and keep me from drinking. Neither she nor Tommy understood how I managed to get drunk each day; they did not know that I would call one of my brothers or sisters and have them deliver a bottle to the back door or hide it in the garbage pail.

One of the psychiatrists who was treating Mae's "problem" finally admitted her to a hospital for a one-month stay. Mae weighed less than 90 pounds, and she convinced the doctor that in order for her to gain weight, she would need "a light drink" before dinner. The doctor gave her permission to keep a bottle in her room, not realizing that Mae's sister was replacing the empty bottle with a full one nearly every day.

Mae happened to see the movie *I'll Quit Tomorrow* with Susan Hayward during her stay in the hospital, and it was through this film that she first began to consider Alcoholics Anonymous. When she was released from the hospital, she called A.A. and actually attended several meetings, but she didn't believe that she "fit in."

It was too degrading and too shameful for me at first. There were very few meetings at that time, and there was only one other woman in the group. To make matters worse, Tommy understood less about A.A. than I did. He was very ashamed that his wife had resorted to "being with drunks," and he declared that he was sure there were no other women at these meetings—he had the only drunk wife in Aberdeen. I had very little self respect left by this time, but at least I was able to tell him that there was one other woman there—it was a very small comfort. By this time, ten of the 11 Ashley children were exhibiting

100

symptoms of alcoholism. I had no idea what was wrong with us, but I was convinced that my drinking was being caused by my unhappy marriage.

Tommy and I were no longer functioning as a married couple: We blamed each other for our problems, hurt each other, used Alex as a pawn, all the things that unhappy people do when they don't understand what is wrong and therefore don't know how to solve their problems. More and more often, Tommy was threatening to send Alex to live with his family in Pittsburgh. I didn't want that to happen, but given the fact that I was drinking more and more heavily, it was only a matter of time before I could no longer care for Alex.

Mae's alcoholism was, quite literally, destroying her and her family. The meetings that she had begun to attend helped her to understand that she was not alone, but she was still unable to overcome the belief that had been so deeply ingrained in her throughout her childhood—that her drinking was her own fault. As a result, Mae remembers that she "struggled with sobriety," going for a week or two without a drink, but then falling back into the same pattern, with the same disastrous results.

Mae Abraham still remembers the precise details and circumstances surrounding her last drinking spree. The incident reflects the way Mae's alcoholism had distorted her ability to reason and function. Mae's sister, Grace, and her husband were both alcoholics, and when Grace's husband died at the age of 44 of his disease, Grace was unable to care for her four children. They were placed in foster care while Grace went to live with Mae. "Talk about the blind leading the blind," Mae recalls. In 1964 Mae arranged for Grace's oldest child, Peyton, who was 13 at the time, to leave foster care and live with her; Mae and Tommy became Peyton's legal guardians.

Soon after Peyton arrived, Mae, Grace, Alex, and Peyton drove to Rehoboth Beach, a popular Delaware resort, for a week's vacation. Mae had recently been released from yet another hospital "rest cure," and the doctor had recommended a change of scenery. Mae still remembers the doctor's precise words to her: "What you need is some fresh air and exercise." Mae persuaded Tommy to let Grace and Peyton accompany her and Alex, "for company," promising (as always) not to drink. Mae still remembers the way that she behaved when they arrived at the motel.

> Grace and I had already started drinking in the car, and when we arrived toward evening, we checked in at the motel, had dinner and a few more drinks, and then went upstairs to unpack. Peyton and Alex were perfectly happy to watch television while Grace and I went out for "a nightcap." That nightcap lasted until four or five in the morning. I drank so much that I had several blackouts, and because I was in a strange town, I couldn't find the motel where we had left the children. I still shudder at the danger I inflicted, not only on my son, but also on Peyton.
>
> When we finally made our way back to the motel, the sun was rising, and instead of feeling relief that the children were safe, I just headed for the bathroom where I was violently ill for the next ten hours.

When Mae returned home, she was "sicker than [she] had ever been." She had always reacted violently to alcohol, but this time, she not only experienced excruciating withdrawal symptoms, she was hallucinating as well. She heard voices and music coming from all areas of the house, and she was convinced that she was dying. Tommy called the family doctor who referred Mae to a psychiatrist, Dr. Adam van Savage.

In August of 1964, shortly after the Rehoboth Beach incident, one of the men in Mae's group suggested they attend a lecture at Johns Hopkins University by Governor Harold Hughes of Iowa.

(Hughes had been a truck driver, and after he overcame his alcoholism, he entered politics and was elected governor. He would later be elected a United States senator.)

Mae decided to attend and got a ride to Johns Hopkins with several members of her group. As she stood in line waiting to go into the auditorium, however, she overheard someone saying there had been a death in Governor Hughes's family, and at the last moment they'd had to find a substitute speaker. Mae still remembers her reaction when she heard that Hughes would not be speaking:

> I asked the person behind me in line who would be speaking instead, and he said that they had gotten a Catholic priest to fill in. I was so upset and disgusted that if I could have, I would have walked home. As a Southern Baptist, I still had absolutely no use whatsoever for Catholic priests, and even worse, I associated the word priest with sermon—every clergyman I had visited during my ten years of drinking had done nothing but given me a sermon about how if I prayed hard enough and long enough, the good Lord would help me to mend my ways. I just had to get right with God, come to church, be a Christian, believe—I had heard it all.
>
> Well, the last thing I needed that evening was another lecture, from a Catholic priest no less. But I had no choice, and I resigned myself to another long-winded sermon.

Instead, Mae Abraham heard Father Martin deliver his Blackboard Talk. Her response was immediate—and permanent. Mae Abraham stopped drinking on the evening she heard Father Martin's presentation, and she has not had another drink since. Despite years of seeking help from "professionals," Mae had never heard the disease of alcoholism described so clearly or so logically before. "From the moment the speaker came out and said, 'Hello, I'm Father Martin, and I'm an alcoholic,'" Mae recalls,

I sensed that I was in the presence of someone who knew and understood me. Everyone had been describing my drinking in terms of a problem with morality: I was evil, sinful, immoral, women don't behave this way. That night, hearing Father Martin's Blackboard Talk, I could see clearly—for the first time—that I did have a problem, but it wasn't a problem with morality, it was a problem with a disease. I looked at the symptoms Father had written on the board and suddenly it became so logical to me, so apparent to me: I had a disease. I felt a tremendous sense of relief and gratitude as I realized that I could accept myself in that way. I walked out of that auditorium vowing that I would never again let anyone make me ashamed of my disease or myself again.

It was the beginning of a new life for me. No one would ever give me a lecture about morality again; no one would ever tell me what was wrong with me again. Now, I would tell them: I have the disease of alcoholism. My attendance at Father's Blackboard Talk was the miracle that saved my life.

I went home that evening and told Tommy what I had heard and how it had changed me; then I called my father and told him that he'd better be prepared for what he was about to hear: a Catholic priest had just saved my life.

Mae's response to Father Martin's Blackboard Talk was similar to the response of hundreds of other people who had heard him speak over the previous six years. Although Father Martin's reputation was growing, and although he was delivering his talk to more and more audiences (sometimes three or four in one week), he never lost the high-spiritedness and spontaneity that made him so popular and effective. Despite these qualities, however, his talk was grounded in a deep understanding of the disease: the result of his own experiences with alcoholism, coupled with the information and wisdom he had gained from Austin Ripley and Dr. Walter Green and augmented by reading, research, and attendance at scores of meetings.

Mae Abraham and Father Martin began their friendship in A.A.: Mae would often call him to ask him for clarification about one of the Steps or how she could deal more effectively with someone in her group, and she thought nothing of driving 30 or 40 miles to bring a new member of the group to hear Father's talk. Then, on the first anniversary of her sobriety, she contacted Father to ask if he would give the Blackboard Talk for her group at St. Joan of Arc parish in Aberdeen. Father said yes, of course. He would never refuse an opportunity to help fellow recovering alcoholics, and since his teaching duties at St. Charles had been greatly reduced by this time, he had more and more time available to do so.

As time passed, the friendship developed; however, Father never actually visited Mae's home. Rather, he learned about Tommy and Alex (who was nine years old at the time), by hearing Mae talk about them. Father and Mae corresponded primarily through letters during this period. These letters reflect not only their deepening friendship, but the way that Mae's knowledge of the Twelve Steps was intensifying. "I'm happy that things are picking up for you," Father wrote to Mae in March of 1967. "Nothing can undo what's been done, but we measure our own bigness in terms of how we adjust to our crosses. You're doing the job, dear, well and in the right way. The rewards will be—must be—great indeed." Mae's mother had recently died, and Mae had asked Father to pray for her mother's soul. "It will be a privilege indeed to do that for you," Father assured Mae.

Father recognized himself—and many other recovering alcoholics—in Mae's behavior, but he soon realized that Mae was devoting an extraordinary amount of time and energy to helping others recover. "She was taking every alcoholic in the county under her wing," Father recalls, "with great energy and love. I was afraid that she was working too hard and would make herself ill from exhaustion. Little did I know that Mae was not like anyone

I had ever met before—or ever would meet—she had more energy and love to give than 20 other people."

In a letter dated February 4, 1966, Father tried to help Mae understand that although working with other alcoholics was essential and admirable, she could not forget that she had to think of herself and her family first.

> Your letter was so very welcome, Mae, but one thing you must (and I feel sure you will) learn is how to allot your time and energies. Oftentimes recovering alcoholics go all out for suffering alcoholics. The reason is an all-consuming gratitude. One thing we must ever bear in mind is the foremost slogan A.A. places in our minds, "First Things First." A.A. restored us to our proper place in life and equipped us to take up and handle our duties and obligations as normal adults. These (usually family and job) come first. Then, and only then, do we husband our time and efforts for others.
>
> Oftentimes my worry about whether I'm giving too much or not enough time to helping alcoholics will be dispelled if I adopt that one guiding principle. Enough.

This same letter contains Father Martin's congratulations to Mae Abraham on the occasion of her and Tommy's conversion to Catholicism. Mae had been deeply influenced not only by Father Martin but by the priests at St. Joan of Arc Parish, where her group met. They had befriended her, counseled her, and supported and praised her recovery. In fact, they often baby-sat for Alex while Mae attended meetings or helped another alcoholic.

On July 21, 1966, Father Martin wrote a letter to Mae to further clarify the advice he had given her on the phone the night before. Mae had called him in a panic; she had been trying (unsuccessfully) to help two alcoholic priests whom she had befriended. One of the priests had arrived at her house "in a very sorry state." Mae was unable to handle him, so she called the rectory where he lived and asked one of the other priests to come and offer assistance. The second priest arrived drunker than the first.

Unable to control her anger and frustration, Mae finally called Father Martin, and as she recalls, "blurted everything that I was feeling out to him."

> I told him that I had never in my life seen a Baptist behave this way; what was it with these Catholic priests? I had one on the couch in my living room and another half kneeling and half lying on the floor next to him, and neither could understand a word one was saying to the other, and I couldn't understand what either of them was saying to me. They both got dreadfully sick in front of Tommy and Alex who just looked at me in absolute horror at the scene that was unfolding in our house. Poor Father Martin—he really bore the brunt of my frustration that night. We laugh about it now, but it certainly wasn't funny then.

"I was disturbed by your call last night," Father wrote to Mae the very next morning:

> I'll give you one rule to follow, Mae, and I'll make it brief. Don't let either one in if he's drinking. Keep this—to the letter. As long as one person will continue to pick up the pieces—the drinking will go on. Let the other priests handle them. If not—that's not your worry. It'll be hard to do but do it.
>
> And don't lose faith. You won't. Yours will only be strengthened. It's a compliment to your faith that God tests it so thoroughly. Here as elsewhere, principles, not persons are important. (But that must be properly understood.) Persons are the important thing—always. But we must know how to handle them. And it differs with circumstances. Hope this all makes sense.

Call again when you've time and we'll talk about it. Pray for me as I do for you. Love to Tom and Alex.

Although their letters contain numerous references to meetings and to principles of recovery, there is ample evidence of the deep respect that was developing between Mae and Father. Frequent references to Tommy and Alex attest to Father's concern for the happiness and well being not only of Mae but of her family as well.

Mae had begun to give Alex the time and attention he had been deprived of because of her alcoholism, and Alex was beginning to thrive both at home and at school. Mae had finally begun to separate her marital problems from her drinking problems, and although it took her a long time to convince Tommy that she was recovering, they began to be friends again. Whenever Mae passed such news along to Father Martin in her letters, he would respond with words of joy and encouragement—just as Austin Ripley had done in his letters to Father during his first few years of recovery.

And in every letter, Father thanked Mae for her "gift," or for her "generosity." In one letter, Father wrote: "My thanks, Mae, for your kind thoughtfulness. Your gift came in mighty handy—you'll never know—and I want you to know it was and is much appreciated. I use the green freely and I think generously, and it is the generosity of a few like yourself who make it possible. Thank you, dear."

"Just a note to thank you ever so much for your ever constant and oh-so-typical thoughtfulness at Christmas," Father wrote to Mae on January 4, 1967. "I'll soon be out of the red."

Father would never have told Mae—or anyone else for that matter—that the only money he had at his disposal during this period, when his teaching duties had been reduced and he had not yet begun to serve as chaplain for the nuns, was the small fee he received each week for assisting at St. William's Parish in Baltimore. Because Father was not teaching, he was not receiving a salary from the Sulpicians. But Mae Abraham possesses a special sense: she knows, intuitively, what other people need—without having to be told. And, she possesses the kindness of spirit that spurs her to respond to those needs, expecting nothing in return. "Goodness for goodness's sake" is the way that Father has described Mae's nature.

It is not surprising then that, in 1970, Father Martin, confused and depressed, and believing that he could not go on living as he was, called Mae Abraham; she was the only one he felt he could trust, he recalls. She could barely understand what he was saying because he was crying into the phone. "I may not have known what time it was," Father recalls, "and I may not have known what I needed, and I was so confused that I may not have known what I was saying, but I did know that if anyone could help me, it was Mae."

Father was right, of course. Mae and Tommy were so worried about Father's state of mind that, although it was long past midnight, Tommy offered to get dressed and drive the hour to Baltimore to get Father and bring him out to their home. After a few minutes' conversation, however, Father assured them that he could make it through the night and that he would think about their invitation to spend a few days resting at their home.

The next day, his young friend, Stu Bramble, drove Father Martin and his German shepherd, Casey, to Mae and Tommy's house in Havre de Grace. (After the death of Father's first dog, Val, he had acquired another German shepherd and named him Casey.) As the car pulled into the Abrahams' driveway, Father suddenly realized that he had no right to expect these people to take care of him. He had never been to their home; he had met Tommy only once or twice. Yet here he was, approaching their front door with a suitcase and a dog. Father suddenly realized what a serious imposition he would be; these people had their own lives to live. But within seconds of arriving at the Abraham home, Father felt comfortable, secure, and wanted. "Welcome to our home," Tommy Abraham said to Father as he reached out his hand. "If it hadn't been for you, we wouldn't have a home."

CHAPTER FIVE

❧

The Chalk Talk

We are told in Hebrews 13:2, "Be not forgetful to entertain strangers, for thereby some have entertained angels unawares." That is the philosophy Mae Abraham had practiced in all of her dealings with alcoholics for the six years of her sobriety, without hesitation, without fanfare, without expecting anything in return. When Mae invited Father Martin to stay with her and her family in 1970, she was doing no more or less for him than she had done for many others.

However, Mae's desire to help Father was inspired not simply by her innate goodness, but by the realization that it was he who had enabled her to find sobriety. Mae had probably "entertained angels unawares" on many occasions, but in this case, she was acutely aware that she was caring for someone very special. "Every time I looked at my little family," Mae recalls, "I said a prayer of thanks to God for bringing Father Martin into my life. So when he called that night, in such terrible shape, I realized that my opportunity to repay him had finally come. There was nothing I wouldn't have done for him."

In fact, Mae went to enormous lengths to help Father. When he first arrived, he was still unable to concentrate for long periods of time. He slept fitfully, suffered from bouts of uncontrollable crying, had little or no appetite, and was convinced, despite Mae and Tommy's protestations, that he had nothing to offer anyone. "I'm 45 years old," he would say to Mae, "and all I have to show for my life is the Blackboard Talk."

Mae remembers telling Father that if he would only get well, one day he would be giving his talk around the world. Little did Mae realize how prophetic her words were. In fact, Mae remembers that she was "scared to death that Father wouldn't get well at all." As she recalls,

> I wanted him to be happy and vital again, not for my sake, not for the sake of others, but for his own sake. Yet, nothing we did seemed to alleviate his depression. I remember there were days when he just wanted to stay in a dark room. He told me that he wanted to sleep, saying, "I didn't realize I was so tired."

Although Father remained withdrawn for the most part, he was immediately drawn to Alex, who was 14 years old at the time. Alex had been told so many times by his parents of Father's influence on his mother's sobriety that he was happy to finally meet him. And by this time, Alex had grown quite accustomed to having "unexpected guests" in his house. As Alex would walk through the living room on his way upstairs, he'd say or do something to make Father laugh. But then, a few moments later, as Alex would again walk past him, the same man who had just been joking with him would be crying or staring vacantly. Alex would ask his mother: "What's wrong with him now?" Mae tried to explain in words that a 14-year-old boy could understand, but "to be honest," Mae recalls,

> I didn't know what was wrong with him either. I knew he had not been drinking; there was no question of that. And I was only vaguely aware of the problems he was encountering as a result of the changes being made at the seminary. Without a teaching appointment for four years, he was wasting his time and life at St. Mary's Seminary on Paca Street in Baltimore, a cavernous old building meant to house hundreds, but now home to about nine priests.

Father had lost all sense of self, that was apparent to me, but how could I explain that to Alex? I told him, as simply as I could, that Father was very depressed.

I think Alex understood far more than I gave him credit for, because he soon began to spend time with Father, asking if he could get him anything. And as the weather grew warmer, Father would sit by the pool and watch Alex and his friends swim. Even in his deeply depressed state, Father still loved to be around young people.

Mae soon realized that she couldn't help Father on her own. Tommy was cooperative and supportive, but he was still working long hours at the restaurant. As a result, Mae called on several A.A. members from Baltimore, people who knew and loved Father. Phil Trischler, an old and valued friend, arranged to come and stay with him for a week. Mae recalls,

He took Father for walks, to meetings, to visit friends. I also called two other friends, an older couple named Veronica and Frank Moore, and they began to visit and talk with him. They were old enough to be his parents, and I think Father enjoyed their wisdom and serenity. Randy Hall, another member of Father's group in Baltimore came, and I remember how devastated Randy felt when he saw how depressed and dispirited Father looked. We had always looked to him for support, guidance, and inspiration. Now, he needed support, guidance, and inspiration himself, and we weren't sure how to give it to him.

Stu Bramble also visited regularly; he just dropped everything to help Father. And it was one afternoon when Stu and I were talking to him that Father happened to mention the pills that he had been taking for his depression. Father told us that perhaps he would call the doctor who

113

had prescribed them because they didn't seem to be working. It was the first time I had even heard that he was on medication, and Stu and I suddenly realized that it was possible that he was responding to drugs in the same way he had responded to alcohol.

When we raised this possibility with Father, he seemed surprised at first. It simply had not occurred to him that something that had been prescribed as a medication could be causing such a profound and negative reaction. "I'll do anything to stop feeling this way," Father said. "Throw the pills away." Even after he stopped taking the medication, however, it took a long time for him to come out of his depression. He still did not express much interest in anything, and he had absolutely no energy. Any type of physical activity left him exhausted.

Mae never lost patience—or hope. "I just kept talking to him and praying to God," she recalls. "I didn't know what else to do." Each evening, Tommy would come home from work and ask Father how he was doing. As months went by, however, Tommy finally confronted Mae. "He's not getting any better; you're not doing anyone any good just letting him stay here like that." Mae told Tommy to be patient, that Father needed time to rest, but Tommy realized that Mae was letting her admiration for Father Martin interfere with plain old common sense.

"Tommy finally sat me down," Mae recalls, "and as gently as he could, he explained that he had meant it when he said that Father was welcome to stay in our home, but he was not welcome to hide in our home." Mae was incredulous. "What do you mean?" She asked Tommy.

"The man needs something to do," Tommy replied. "Everyone around here has heard of Father Martin, and they love and respect him. When they hear he's a guest at my house, they treat me as if I've got a celebrity under my roof. He's got to use those talents, Mae. He can't go on like this. If he does, he'll die, and you know it."

Mae began to realize that Tommy was right, and as Father Martin recalls, "she went into action, and when Mae gets it into her head to do something, she does it."

Mae started with the dogs. Alex had a Norwegian elkhound named Heidi who was almost as poorly behaved as Father's German shepherd, Casey. Mae sent the four of them—Father, Alex, and the two dogs—to a canine-training class. "That's how we started to get Father driving again and out of the house," Mae recalls. "No one's behavior improved very much, but they had a lot of fun."

Next, Mae helped Father "get his affairs in order." Now that he was no longer a member of the Sulpician society, he was, as a diocesan priest, required to function with the approval and support of the Archbishop of Baltimore, his home diocese. In this case, it was Archbishop William Borders, a gentle and kind man who quickly became one of Father's strongest supporters. Archbishop Borders gave Father Martin permission to reside with the Abrahams provided that he had adequate privacy and that his living arrangements did not interfere with his ability to perform his priestly functions.

With Father's personal affairs in order, and with his health and energy slowly returning, Mae set about finding him something to do to support himself. "I didn't have the slightest idea how to go about this," Mae recalls,

> but I was sure of one thing. Father Martin knew more about alcoholism than anyone I knew or knew of, and at about this time I learned that the state of Maryland had become the first state in the nation to inaugurate a Division of Alcoholism Control. I called them immediately, and spoke to Riley Regan, whom Father and I knew.
>
> The division had been in operation for less than a year, and I asked Riley if he had a need for a lecturer. I still remember the way my heart was

beating. This would be the perfect position for Father, and if he didn't get a job with this agency, I didn't have any other place to turn. Riley said that if he had known Father was available, he would have called and offered him a job immediately. Riley had simply assumed that Father would be far too busy—and was far too prominent—to even consider such an offer. We set up an appointment for Father to go to the office and complete the necessary paperwork, and as soon as I hung up the phone, I said a very long prayer of thanks to God.

Father would be working with an Episcopal priest and former lawyer named Harry Shelly, and with a social worker named Gertrude Nilsson, conducting day-long seminars for doctors, lawyers, parole officers, and social workers employed by the state of Maryland. Gertrude Nilsson still remembers the joy she felt "the moment Father Martin signed his employment papers" and officially became an employee of the Division of Alcoholism Control. The agency was one of the first of its kind in the United States, and "to be honest," she recalls, "none of us were very sure of what we were supposed to be doing."

In fact, it was Gertrude Nilsson, whose primary experience had been working in the field of mental health, who had helped to create the Comprehensive Alcoholism Law of the State of Maryland. Passed in July of 1968, the law shifted alcoholism from the judicial realm to the realm of public health. Recognizing that alcoholism is a disease, not a criminal act, it stated that a person could not be arrested for displaying in public the symptoms of an illness. As a result of this law, there was suddenly a pressing need for education for state employees and for treatment facilities for alcoholics. "I had seen so many alcoholics being dumped into mental-health facilities where their alcoholism wasn't even dealt with, much less treated," Nilsson recalls.

But when the state finally recognized the problem and set up an agency to do something about it, there were very few people who had the proper training and experience to educate both alcoholics and non-alcoholics.

Hiring Father Martin was the key to our success. Here was a man who could speak from experience: other alcoholics could trust him, and non-alcoholics could learn from him. And of equal importance was his extraordinary ability as a communicator. He could work a crowd like no one I had ever seen. Of all the things I did in the field of alcoholism recovery in my long career, the thing that I am still most proud of is having the good sense (and the good luck) to work with Father Joseph Martin.

Suddenly, Father was being paid to do the same thing he had been doing for several years. "It felt good to be able to support myself," he recalls.

I was traveling all over Maryland with Gertrude; with Riley Regan, who went on to direct the Division of Alcoholism for the New Jersey Department of Health; and with Father Harry Shelly, a lawyer who had become an Episcopal priest. I learned so much from them, and all four of us began to realize just how important our work was. Very few people actually understood the disease of alcoholism; very often, our presentations marked the first occasion that people heard alcoholism described as a disease. So it was very rewarding.

The state sent me to the famous Summer School of Alcohol Studies at Rutgers University in June and July of 1970. It helped me get a better understanding of the kind of training that was beginning to be offered to counselors and educators. I certainly never considered myself a "professional" in the field, but I did realize that I had got-

ten a very good grounding during my months at
Guest House with Rip and Doc Green.

The fact that Father Martin wore a Roman collar while pre-
senting his talk actually enhanced the quality of his presentation.
"He engendered a great deal of respect during his talks,"
Gertrude Nilsson recalls.

> When he stood up and said, in front of audiences,
> that he was an alcoholic, they were absolutely
> floored. Their preconceived notions about alco-
> holics, many of them still used the word "drunks,"
> did not include a Catholic priest who was articu-
> late, engaging, handsome, and joyful. He was a
> very effective speaker. We were an instant success
> because of Father's charisma, knowledge, and tal-
> ent; he was a real boon to Maryland's program.

By this time, Father Martin's "visit" to the Abrahams had
evolved into a comfortable, happy, and permanent living arrangement. Although the Abrahams would continue to call him Father
Martin, both out of habit and respect, a deep sense of affection
and trust soon developed. Tommy and Father began to "putter
around in the kitchen," an arrangement that pleased Mae enormously. Father's income from the state of Maryland was not large,
but it was certainly ample for his needs.

Alex and Father grew even closer; in fact, Alex grew so comfortable having Father in the house that he would often say, "I'm
lucky; I've got a Mom, a Dad, and a Father."

By early 1971, Father was convinced that the period he has
described as "one of the worst times I've ever endured" had finally ended. His mental, spiritual, and emotional condition was so
improved that he wrote to Austin Ripley to assure him that his
"crisis" was finally over and to inform Ripley about his new job
and living arrangements. As always, Ripley responded with great
enthusiasm and insight.

"What a joy it was to receive your sincere, vibrant, and opti-
mistic letter," Ripley responded.

Though never having been a victim of it, except for brief, temporary times, I sympathize deeply with those who have undergone the utter spiritual desolation of depression. Its intense suffering is so subtle, so heavy-footed, that one appears simply unable to summon his own inner resources to master it. The fact that you were able to honestly confront yourself, admit your pill addiction, and receive, through the grace of God, such warm and friendly help from the Abrahams, resulted in your magnificent breakthrough. I share deeply with you, Father Joe, the joys of your victory.

The consequences of your heavy involvement in the field of alcoholism indeed must result in great inner rewards and deep satisfaction of the spirit. How happy I am that you who have so very much to offer others now have the singular opportunity of so doing.

Father Martin began to assist on weekends at St. Joan of Arc Parish, the parish to which the Abrahams belonged, and he soon got to know the parishioners there. It did not take people very long to realize that he was always available to them if they needed help—or if they wanted to hear a funny story. "Everybody loved my jokes but Mae," Father recalls. "If I got even a faint smile from Mae, then I knew I had told a zinger."

Mae suspects that "there may have been some talk" about the fact that a priest was living in their home, "but nothing they said about Father Martin could have compared with the talk that must have gone on when my drinking was out of control," Mae recalls, "so I just went about my business. Father was getting better, and Tommy and Alex loved having him in our home. That's all I cared about. I certainly wasn't going to worry about what other people thought."

Mae does remember one amusing incident that occurred when she and Father were asked to speak about alcoholism to a group of Episcopal women at Father Harry Shelly's parish in Baltimore.

> Father Harry got up and introduced me as "the woman that Father Martin lives with." There was dead silence, and Father Shelly turned purple. I stood up and told the women that although it was true that Father Martin lived with me, my husband and son lived with me as well. There was a very audible sigh of relief from the audience, followed by laughter.

It was at about this time that Mae decided to add a bedroom and bathroom to the house so that Father Martin would have even more privacy. "We were sitting in the backyard one day," Father recalls,

> and Tommy and I noticed that Mae was staring at the back of the house. A few moments later, she declared that she had solved the problem, and she proceeded to describe her plans for an addition in great detail. Believe it or not, the builder agreed with her completely, and within two months I had my own quarters. The idea of building Ashley hadn't even been conceived yet, but we would eventually realize that Mae was exhibiting her first symptoms of "buildingitis," a term used by Sam Noble, who would become an Ashley benefactor and board member, to describe Mae's propensity for expanding.

At about this time, Mae asked Father Martin if he thought she should take some of the courses that were beginning to be offered on alcoholism. "No," Father replied. "You don't need 'knowledge'; your understanding of alcoholics comes from your heart and your experience." Father's admiration for Mae's devotion to alcoholics continued to grow as he saw, first-hand, the way she responded to their needs. He would often tell people

The Chalk Talk

that Mae was "a true descendant of Bill and Doctor Bob, figuring it out as they went along, but always getting it right."

Early in 1971 Father received a call from a minister mentioning that a friend of his, Leonard Dahl, a Presbyterian minister in the Aberdeen area, would benefit from a call from Father Martin. Leonard still remembers Father's gentle and subtle approach during their first phone conversation.

> He was so wonderful. I remember that he used the words "I hear you may have a problem." He didn't say "You have a drinking problem and need help." His disposition and behavior were so delicate, so easy to accept and respond to. As long as I live, I will remember Father Martin's voice on the telephone saying to me, "I hear you may have a problem. Is there something I can do to help?"

Leonard, Father, and Mae soon became good friends, and for several years, he and Mae attended meetings together. Leonard saw, first-hand, the way that Mae helped other alcoholics.

> It came so naturally to her. I would watch in amazement as Mae communicated with people who were really struggling with their sobriety. I suspect that Mae was so effective because she saw herself reflected in every one of them, and she wanted them to get better so that they could have the joy of sobriety that she was enjoying.

After Leonard's recovery, he sought further training in the field and eventually became the Executive Director of a halfway house for men in Bel Air, Maryland. Even after he accepted a position in Pittsburgh as a Family Therapist and Pastoral Counselor at Gateway, Leonard stayed in touch with Father, Mae, and Tommy. Little did any of them realize at the time what an enormous role Leonard would eventually play in their lives.

Father continued to present his Blackboard Talk for the state of Maryland, driving with Gertrude Nilsson, Harry Shelly, and Riley Regan to sites across the state. The traveling tired him out, and he would often fall asleep in the car, but as Gertrude Nilsson recalls,

> the very presence of an audience would invigo-rate him. His entire countenance would change. It's hard to describe, but there was a certain "elec-tricity" about him—people would sense it and respond to it. I knew very little about the art of effective communication in those days, but I knew when I saw Father Martin that something extraordinary was happening to the audience. It never failed; within five minutes of the beginning of his talk, people would be leaning forward in their chairs, laughing, nodding in agreement, pay-ing close and careful attention.
>
> When he'd finished, the lines would begin to form. People would want to talk to Father, ask him questions, get his autograph, even touch him. By then, he would be exhausted, and often we would have to leave quickly to get to our next speaking engagement, but no matter how tired or rushed he was, Father Martin never exhibited signs of impatience or exhaustion. He may have been effective talking to a crowd of people, but he knew that the crowd was comprised of individu-als, and he cared very much about each of them, particularly those who were in the early stages of recovery.

Father Martin continued to maintain contact with Austin Ripley through yearly visits and regular correspondence. Ironically, at about this time, their fortunes began to reverse. Father Martin's recovery—under the loving care of Mae Abraham—was complete, and his ability to help alcoholics through his Blackboard Talks was becoming recognized more and more widely. However, late in 1969, the board of directors of Guest House had been forced to ask Austin Ripley for his resig-nation. He had worked so hard, for so long, that his performance and behavior had begun to be affected, and the board feared not only for the future of Guest House, but for Ripley's health.

Ripley did take the long rest that the board recommended, and although he did not resume his duties as Director of Guest House, he did re-establish a good relationship with the board members. By early 1970 Ripley had come up with yet another plan, to establish a facility for nuns modeled on Guest House, to be called Pilgrim House. However, he encountered the very same resistance from Church officials that he had when he originally conceived of Guest House.

Father's belief in Ripley's project, coupled with the affection and respect he felt for his good friend, led him to offer to help in any way he could, writing to those Superiors whom he knew asking them to help. On one occasion when Ripley visited the Baltimore area, Father Martin did everything to make Ripley's stay as enjoyable as possible, including lunch at a restaurant chosen especially by Father because it served wonderful crab cakes. Ripley wrote to Father Martin when he returned to Wisconsin to express his gratitude:

> How can I thank you, Father Joe, for your gracious kindness and the unlimited time you spent with me and the number of trips you made taking me to my various appointments? Do you know that I am deeply grateful for this generous evidence of friendship?
>
> It was just great seeing you again in such excellent health and spirits. You got it! The fact that you have warms my heart. And that delightful luncheon! The very finest crab I have ever had.

Father continued to help Austin Ripley in any way that he could, but Father could not help noticing that Ripley's strength and health had deteriorated. "He was as brilliant and stubborn as ever," Father Martin recalls, "but I realized that age was catching up with him. He didn't seem to realize it though, and was as indefatigable as ever, willing to take on whoever came between him and his determination to help nuns in the same way he had helped so many of us priests."

At about the same time that Father Martin began his work with the state of Maryland, the United States Congress passed the Comprehensive Alcohol Abuse and Prevention Treatment and Rehabilitation Act, largely as a result of the efforts of Harold Hughes of Iowa. (It was Governor Harold Hughes who had been scheduled to speak at Johns Hopkins on that evening in August of 1964 when Mae traveled to Baltimore with members of her group, but because of a death in Hughes's family, Father Martin had been asked to replace him.) Hughes was now a senator representing the state of Iowa, and his tireless efforts, combined with a deep understanding of alcoholism—a result of his own experiences—had led him to crusade for the passage of an act insuring that the disease of alcoholism would be dealt with nationally, in both the private and public sector.

Under the auspices of the Department of Health, Education, and Welfare, the National Institute of Alcohol Abuse and Alcoholism was formed. It would provide services and instruction on a national basis similar to those that Maryland had been providing at the state level. The federal government directed that all federal employees receive two hours of alcohol and drug education each year.

As a direct result of this directive, Father Martin was asked to give his Blackboard Talk to a group of about 75 people representing various government agencies as part of a day-long seminar at the Federal Building in Washington, D.C. Two officers, Jim McMahon and Dale Geiger, both commanders in the U.S. Navy, attended the seminar in search of educational material to fulfill the new educational directives, and they were so impressed with Father's presentation that they asked him if they could film it. McMahon, a Lieutenant Commander and one of the Deputy Program Managers for Alcohol Education who had seen and heard Father Martin many times and who had been placed in charge of creating educational material, recalls,

All of the armed services had a problem with alcoholism, and the Navy was no exception. The military was always known as a heavy-drinking population, and there was a certain macho image that many of the sailors embraced. Heavy drinking was perceived as a sign of strength. There was an expression in those days, "In order to fly with the eagles you had to be able to hoot with the owls."

Furthermore, conditions were rife for drinking: New recruits were away from home, often for the first time, away from the usual support systems of family and church. Loneliness and a desire to be included often led them to partying and drinking. Booze as the great lubricator. We had no material, no information, no resources that could effectively counteract these behaviors and attitudes.

So when I heard that Father Martin was to speak at a conference right in my backyard, I grabbed Dale Geiger, another newly sober Commander, and headed for the conference, along with a Navy photographer. When I asked if we could film the Blackboard Talk, Father Martin said, "Be my guest."

Father did not give the taping very much thought: After all, he had been presenting the Blackboard Talk for 12 years. He had presented the earliest version of the talk soon after he returned to Baltimore from Guest House, and he had delivered it hundreds of times since then, before small groups, in front of large audiences such as the one at Johns Hopkins where Mae had first heard him, and most recently, all over the state of Maryland as an employee of the Division of Alcoholism Control. He was simply doing what he had always done: talking about alcoholism to whomever would listen—for their sake, and for his own.

Jim McMahon had only recently begun his own recovery from alcoholism, and he remembers being "absolutely floored" the first time he heard Father's Blackboard Talk.

> I knew immediately that I was witnessing a very special event. Here was a man who wasn't preaching or lecturing; he was speaking from the heart, with "just the facts, ma'am." There was an authenticity about his talk, a sincerity and honesty that helped me see the truth of what he was saying. There were the jokes of course, tasteful and relevant. And there was an intellectual component as well; Father engaged in an intellectual process and allowed you to engage in it with him, to follow the logic and reasoning and clarity of his argument, one step at a time.

McMahon and Geiger were excited about the film. They had it developed immediately and brought it to their supervisor at the Pentagon, Captain Jim Baxter. "I had no doubt that Baxter would be as impressed as I was," McMahon recalls. "It was the most effective teaching tool about alcoholism that I had ever seen; it was as simple as that."

However, Baxter was, according to McMahon, "decidedly underwhelmed." Father Martin still remembers the account that McMahon provided of the conversation that ensued:

> Baxter: "What have you got here?"
>
> McMahon: "A Catholic priest."
>
> Baxter: "Strike one."
>
> McMahon: "He stands in front of a blackboard and writes on it and lectures."
>
> Baxter: "Strike two."
>
> McMahon: "The film runs well over an hour and a half."
>
> Baxter: "Strike three."

Baxter asked Commander John Frederick, whose job it was to make films to promote Navy enlistment, to take a look at the tape. McMahon remembers that Frederick wasn't impressed either, because he "let his very extensive knowledge of film-making affect his evaluation of the efficacy of the film." One could hardly blame Frederick; even someone with little or no knowledge of film-making would recognize instantly that the sound and lighting were poor, there was only one angle (only one camera had been used), and there was no music. Frederick insisted that the film would never sell, but he did admit that he could be wrong, telling McMahon and Geiger that he hadn't thought *The Godfather* would be a success either.

McMahon and Geiger listened to the criticism, but they knew that the quality of the film was not what mattered. What mattered was Father Martin's performance. All fine lectures are actually performances, and Father Martin's performance during the taping of his talk was spell-binding (just as it always had been, and just as it continues to be).

During the taping, Father spoke with a clear, rich, pleasing voice, and his timing was impeccable. He had grown up during the radio era, and while he may have learned about alcoholism from his own experiences, from Austin Ripley and Dr. Walter Green, and from reading and research, his ability to speak so effectively about alcoholism was a direct result of the hours and hours he had spent as a child listening to—and imitating—his favorite comedians telling jokes and stories.

Father's appearance was also a factor in the success of the Chalk Talk (the title the Navy began to use, permanently replacing "Blackboard Talk"). The film was made in 1972, when Father Martin was 48 years old. His red hair had turned silver, but it was still thick and wavy. His complexion was clear, he was vigorous and lively, and his black suit and white Roman collar lent him an air of authority. Father Martin never lectured or preached to his audience; in this sense, the title "Chalk Talk" is particularly accurate. He is a master of "plain speech," that simple prose for which Abraham Lincoln is so admired. But all experts in the field of communication know that economical and precise prose is the result of an extraordinarily complex process of thinking and preparing. Father Martin was able to speak plainly to his audience because he had developed the ability to simplify complex ideas without reducing them to clichés. Father engaged in a system of thinking that he learned in the seminary: the central proposition of the Chalk Talk was the disease of alcoholism—everything else defined, explained, and supported that proposition.

Father never forgot what Austin Ripley once told him: one of the first things to return with sobriety is a sense of humor—and Father was determined to share his wonderful sense of humor with all those with whom he came in contact. He told several jokes throughout the talk; they were funny, tasteful, and relevant. Father knew that he was dealing with a most serious topic, but he also knew that "when tragedy is the subject, if you don't laugh, you cry."

Father spoke to his audience as if he were engaged in a conversation with them, explaining or clarifying his ideas and theories by writing notes on the chalkboard. He made it all look so effortless, speaking for a few moments, offering examples and evidence, and then jotting down a key word or phrase on the board—while still talking. In actuality, however, he was performing a skill that very few possess. While writing the word or phrase that he had just mentioned on the board, he continued his conversation. As a result, he was writing a different word or phrase than the one he was speaking, a skill he had developed during his many years of teaching.

Furthermore, in all of his actions and movements, one is reminded of Hal Tulley's description of Father Martin's quick grace when he used to enter his classroom, and using the pointer and his cape, execute a perfect *arruzzina* to attract the attention of the students. During the Chalk Talk, after erasing several words and phrases from the board, Father finished his sentence, and as if to accentuate the point he had just made, held the eraser up near his face and blew away the chalk dust that had accumulated. The analogy was immediately apparent to everyone:

one's life can be blown away by alcoholism as quickly as the chalk dust had just been blown into the air.

Father did not use the chalkboard as most teachers do, simply jotting down a word or phrase. Instead, he used every inch of the board, placing important information, numbered and ordered, in both the right and left upper corners. Then, he wrote words or phrases that he intended to erase in the middle of the board. When he returned to a particular point or topic that he had mentioned earlier, he would also return to the right or left corner of the chalk board and point to the information, thus providing audience members with a visual aid that would help them remember a particular point or make crucial connections.

It is impossible to record the contents of Father's Chalk Talk; in fact, at the beginning of his lectures or at the beginning of a viewing of the film, people frequently try to take notes. They soon realize, however, that it is better simply to sit back and listen: too much is lost in the transposition from the spoken word to the written word. Of course, everything Father says about the disease of alcoholism during his Chalk Talk is of vital importance, however it is the way he communicates the information that makes the material so compelling. (In fact, in 1982, the Chalk Talk and two of his other talks, "Guidelines for Helping Alcoholics" and "Alcoholism and the Family," were put into a book, *No Laughing Matter.* However, simply reading the book deprives the reader of the central part of it all: Father Martin himself.)

Father Martin spoke for one hour and 20 minutes during the Navy's taping session, yet he spoke entirely without notes, never once mispronouncing a word, never once digressing or losing his train of thought. Although Father's talk was memorized (after all, he had been delivering it for almost 15 years), it seemed to emanate from a deep understanding not only of the material but also of the people to whom he was speaking. As he spoke, it became clear to the audience almost immediately that he was not lecturing to them, he was sharing with them knowledge that had been gained from others and from personal experience.

Father Martin ended the Chalk Talk in the same way he always had, by thanking the people in the audience for honoring him by listening to him and for the privilege of spending time with them. And as always, he received a standing ovation.

Burt Frasher, a Commander in charge of the financial end of producing material for the Navy (who had found Father's film helpful in his own recovery) convinced his superiors to let others view the Chalk Talk film. This would be, he argued, the most objective method to determine if the film was effective. He sent copies to each of the five Alcoholism Rehabilitation Centers of the Navy; their evaluations did not contain one negative comment.

Frasher also sent a copy of the tape to Jamie Carraway, the executive director of Fellowship Hall in Greensboro, North Carolina, one of the pre-eminent alcohol-recovery treatment centers in the country at the time. Carraway knew that the real test would be the response of alcoholics who were in treatment at his facility, so he gathered about 50 patients to view the film. Carraway still remembers the response:

> I was a Southern Baptist, and throughout my childhood I had been told that Catholics were evil. So when I heard the film contained a lecture by a Catholic priest, although I had graduated from college and was supposedly "worldly and sophisticated," all those stereotypes I had heard about Catholics returned. But I had agreed to show the film, and I was determined to keep my word.
>
> I stood at the back of the auditorium and watched the patients viewing the film. The response was remarkable. Usually, patients who are in the early stages of recovery have a very difficult time sitting still for long periods of time, but throughout the time the film was being run, not one patient got up to go to the bathroom; there was no shifting and fussing; no one even lit a cigarette.

My own reservations about the film evaporated almost immediately, not just because of the way the patients were responding, but because in all my years of involvement in the field of alcoholism recovery, I had never seen or heard anything so effective, interesting, and inspiring. I began to realize there was something very special about Father Martin; I believed then, and I still believe, that God had touched him and chosen him to explain alcoholism.

At that moment I didn't particularly care what the Navy thought of the film; all I knew was I wanted a copy of it for Fellowship Hall. I realized that the film was accomplishing in one hour what it took us weeks to do, that is, help our patients acquire a thorough understanding of what was wrong with them.

The beauty of the film was the way it crossed all sorts of boundaries: We had people in the audience at all stages of treatment—earliest to latest, and we had people in the audience from all walks of life—from executives to construction workers. Almost everyone responded in the same way. Many of them were crying when the film ended, and I believe they were crying from the sheer relief of finally hearing someone describe to them precisely what was wrong in terms they could understand, without judgment, without preaching, without condescension.

McMahon and Frasher were encouraged by Carraway's response, and they continued to lobby for the use of the film. They decided to use it as part of a four-hour workshop they had put together, a workshop that would include a pre- and post-evaluation to measure the effectiveness of each segment of the workshop. The evaluation indicated unequivocally that the most effective element of the workshop had been the film. And as if

Father Martin, as an "honorary" member of the Armed Forces, delivered the Chalk Talk to thousands of enlisted men and women. (Courtesy of Father Martin.)

that were not enough evidence, one of the people who viewed the tape stood up and declared that he was going to turn himself in for treatment.

Next, Frasher had more copies of the film printed, and using a list of recovered alcoholics who were still enlisted in the Navy, he sent a copy to the 450 people on the list and asked for their opinion. Again, the response was overwhelmingly positive. The only problem was trying to get the copies back: the people to whom he had sent the tapes returned the questionnaire immediately, but most of them said that they wanted to keep the film to show to friends or to watch again and again for inspiration.

Jim McMahon recalls that he and Burt Frasher were finally able to convince their superiors that they "had a winner," and within two months they had 1,800 copies of the film printed, packed in a drug and alcohol education kit, and sent to Navy bases around the world. (The Navy eventually cut the film to slightly more than an hour so that it would fit on one reel. "I understood why they did it," Father recalls, "but they lopped off a couple of really good jokes.")

Father Martin was kept informed of the progress of the film. He was pleased that it was being so well received, and he was aware, of course, that the government owned the film; he had signed a talent release before the filming. The Navy had given Father ten copies of the film. (He and Mae sold them to treatment centers that had heard of the film but could not purchase it because it was not being made available to non-government agencies.) "I wasn't at all worried about money," Father recalls, "but I began to be a little concerned that I would lose my ability to earn a living. If people could see me on film, why would they bother to pay to have me as a speaker?"

The Navy realized that Father certainly deserved some sort of compensation (the film was so well received that requests for more prints were flooding McMahon's office), so they sent Father an honorarium of $2,500. Within months of the initial release of the film, requests for personal appearances started to come from Navy bases all over the United States and then from all over the world. Within a year, Chalk Talk had made Father the most well known and sought-after speaker about alcoholism in the world.

In January of 1974, Father Martin, along with ten Navy officers and three other civilians, traveled to Spain, Italy, and Greece in order to train and educate officers and base commanders about alcoholism. "It was the first time I had ever been outside the United States," Father recalls, "and I was absolutely thrilled."

It was becoming more and more difficult, however, for Father to continue to do his work for the state of Maryland while traveling to various Navy bases, in addition to trying to satisfy the speaking requests that began to pour in from all over the United States. "I still wasn't very concerned about the money, although it was nice to be able to support myself," Father recalls,

> but I was concerned about making commitments that I wouldn't be able to keep. I was being asked to schedule dates six and seven months in advance. So I sat down with Mae and Tommy, and we all agreed that I should resign my job with the state and function on a freelance basis. I remember Tommy joked that if I continued to be so successful, I would soon need an agent. We all laughed, but in a way, I already had an agent, Mae Abraham.
>
> Mae began to help me more and more, arranging my schedule, driving me to and from the airport, helping me with a growing correspondence. All the while, she was still as active as ever in Twelve Step work, and she was still running the house for Tommy and Alex. She had an enormous supply of energy and enthusiasm.

Mae also had an enormous supply of common sense. She soon began to realize that Father could not sustain such a grueling travel schedule: in the years following the filming of the Chalk Talk, he spoke in all 50 states, and in more than 20 countries, sometimes spending weeks at a time in one country speaking at

Army, Navy, Air Force, and Coast Guard bases in addition to civilian alcoholism and drug facilities.

In time, Mae suggested to Father Martin that he make his own films about other aspects of recovery; in that way he could maintain control over them. "I was excited about the idea," Father recalls. "I felt I could develop more talks on other aspects of this complex thing we call addiction."

Mae suggested borrowing $30,000 from a bank to film "Guidelines" and three other talks, but Father was afraid to make such a large financial commitment. At about this time, John Frederick (the Navy officer who had concluded that Father's Chalk Talk was ineffectual) retired and became a partner in a film production company, F.M.S. Productions, with two other men, Rick Miner and Herman Saunders. (Saunders, the founder of the company, had worked under Jack Webb for 30 years, producing such television series as "Adam-12" and "F Troop.") Frederick called Father to discuss the possibility of producing other films. Mae and Father knew little about film production, and they had very little capital, so they entered into a partnership with F.M.S. Productions. Some of Father's most successful films were produced as a result of this partnership. The films were edited and transferred to videotape for distribution.

One of the first videos Father Martin made under these new arrangements was based on material he had learned from Gertrude Nilsson. Just as Father had used the knowledge he had gained from Austin Ripley and Dr. Walter Green in his Chalk Talk to help recovering alcoholics, so he used the information he had learned from Gertrude. This is not as unusual as it seems at first. Most speakers and writers protect their material with copyrights, believing that they and only they have a right to the "intellectual property" they have produced. Recovering alcoholics have no such compunction, however. If it works, they share it with others—it's as simple as that. However, Father was so scrupulous that he always informed his listeners of the source of his knowledge. For example, in his introduction to the presentation entitled "Guidelines for Helping Alcoholics," Father told his audience:

> Gertrude Nilsson deserves the credit for the following ideas. She began her social work on the Eastern Shore of Maryland, where she worked for 20 years. After a few years, during which Gertrude was very successful in helping alcoholics and their families, her supervisor asked her to write down what she had learned.
>
> Gertrude is a humble person; she was not out to impress anyone. So she wrote her "Ten Commandments" on one side of one piece of paper. They were ten simple declarative sentences that contained the essence of everything she had learned from thousands of people in the field. These commandments of hers are the result of experience: pragmatism at its best.

Father condensed Nilsson's "Ten Commandments" into eight guidelines: Acquire proper attitudes toward the alcoholic; Learn to recognize the disease of alcoholism through a knowledge of the symptoms; Understand that alcoholism is addiction to alcohol; Confront the alcoholic with the fact of the disease; Make the alcoholic responsible for his or her behavior; Get to know the alcoholism resources in your community; Don't get discouraged; Alcoholism is a family disease, and the family needs treatment.

In his presentation, Father elaborated on each guideline, drawing, as always, on the knowledge he had gained from Austin Ripley and Dr. Walter Green and from his own experiences. But in addition, Father was now drawing on the wisdom and knowledge he had gained as a result of traveling around the world meeting and talking with others. Although he still followed the same basic format that he had employed in the Chalk Talk, he now drew on the experiences of the many people he had met. As Father recounted an incident he had heard about in Alaska or as he described an event he had witnessed in Tokyo, his audience was better able to appreciate the universality of the disease of alcoholism—and of the recovery process.

Although Father received royalties from these films, F.M.S. Productions owned the rights to them, and eventually, he and Mae decided it would make more sense to form their own production company. As a result, they founded Kelly Productions (named after one of the Abrahams' dogs), operating it out of the basement of their home. Father remembers that "Mae brought cardboard containers home from the supermarket every time she went grocery shopping, and we would use them to ship the tapes." The business was soon successful enough to enable Mae to hire her sister, Pat Hitchcock, to help with packing and shipping.

However, as Father recalls, the business "soon began to mushroom from the basement into the upstairs rooms." At the time, Tommy still owned a restaurant in Aberdeen, and he offered Mae and Father space in an unused room behind the restaurant. "It was an extraordinary relief," Mae recalls, "to actually have some space to cook and do laundry again." (In addition, Mae began to order packing material, eliminating the need to lug cartons home from the supermarket.)

Alex had begun to travel with Father to some of his speaking engagements at about this time, and he began to notice how frequently the people who greeted Father after his presentation asked for audio or video recordings of the talk he had just given. As a result, Alex began to record Father's talks and convert them into audiotapes; in this way, people who could not afford a videotape could still hear his lectures. The tapes were an instant hit: people purchased them, not only for themselves, but as gifts for friends. As the demand for the tapes increased, Alex decided to hire a professional to make the original recordings and to produce the tapes.

As the popularity of the video- and audiotapes continued to increase, Mae was able to hire more employees. Furthermore, given Mae's highly refined sense of propriety, she realized that, although Archbishop Borders had given Father Martin permission to support himself as a lecturer rather than as a parish priest, people could become suspicious of a priest who was selling tapes and charging lecture fees. People who knew Father and Mae realized they had a staff and a payroll to meet every week, but others would often ask whether Father was turning his profits over to the Church. Mae put Father on salary, just like everyone else in the firm; in that way she helped to dispel any suspicions that Father was pocketing huge sums of money or that the Church was profiting.

Chalk Talk continued to grow in popularity. Dr. Conway Hunter, who had started and directed Peachford Hospital in Atlanta, Georgia, one of the first freestanding hospitals for the treatment of substance abuse, had heard about the tape. He contacted the local Navy headquarters in Atlanta and asked for a copy, but he was informed that the film was "classified," and that it could not be released to civilians. "I wasn't willing to take no for an answer," Conway Hunter recalls, "so I called the commander of the local army headquarters, and that same day, two MPs brought it to the hospital." Chalk Talk was an instant success with the patients, and as a result, Hunter contacted Father Martin and asked him to come to Peachford Hospital to speak to the patients.

In the mid 1970s, when Hunter organized the first Southeastern Conference on Alcohol and Drugs (SECAD), he realized that Father Martin "was the logical choice as the keynote speaker." Dr. Hunter recalls the effect Father Martin had on the audience.

> My goal in starting SECAD had been to educate physicians who were still misdiagnosing and mistreating alcoholics and drug addicts. However, very few doctors actually came to the conference. That really didn't matter, however, because the conference was such a success and had such a positive impact on those who did attend that it became an annual event, and Father Martin became an integral part of it.

He was so charismatic, so warm, so enjoyable to listen to, that the audience couldn't get enough of him. His ability to communicate was an important part of his success, of course, but more than that, it was his ability to speak from experience so honestly. He wasn't telling us what he had learned through reading or through course work; he was telling us what he had learned through his own experience.

My friendship with Father Martin began to grow after that conference. We had recovered at about the same time in our lives, and as we spent time together, I came to understand his devotion to alcoholics. Father is actually a rather shy person—although few people realize this. They see only his humor and intelligence and competence; they don't realize that his eloquence and conviction stems from his need to help others, not from a desire for attention.

I've been active in the field of alcoholism treatment for a very long time, and I know just about everyone who has played a part in its development. So I can judge the effect that Father has had on the field. Whenever I introduce Father, I tell the audience that if they took all of the others and what they've done, and put them on one side of a scale, and if they put Father Martin on the other side of the scale—the scale would tip under his weight. He's an invaluable and irreplaceable resource.

Terry Gorski, another professional who would later achieve great prominence in the field of alcoholism, particularly in the area of relapse treatment, saw Father Martin's Chalk Talk at about this time. He remembers the impact it had on him.

I was exposed to Chalk Talk because it was used as one of the early training films in a course I was taking on chemical dependency at Grant Hospital in Chicago. The film really altered my thinking because of its clarity—it helped me to see how all of these apparently disorganized symptoms of addiction actually contain a conceptual thread that pulls everything together. There are magical moments in communication, and I knew I was witnessing one of them. Father had the ability to communicate very complex concepts of addiction, recovery, and spirituality in extremely clear, simple, easy-to-understand concepts that bring the audience alive.

I was a young, very impressionable student at the time, and I remember thinking, however naively, that I wanted to be able to have the same impact on people that Father Martin had. I could never perform the way he did; I don't mean that sort of impact, I mean the ability to change lives, to help people, to help them feel alive again. That's what Father did through his Chalk Talk.

One cannot ignore the effect of the humor, either. Father Martin is a genuinely funny person and an excellent joke teller. I found this out in a very humorous way. Early in my practice, I had a patient who was just completing detox, and knowing that he was a practicing Catholic, I believed that Father Martin's Chalk Talk could help him with his recovery, even though he still wasn't thinking clearly.

After this patient viewed the tape, I asked him what he thought of it, convinced that he would be as impressed and affected as I was. "Well," he said, "it's a very informative tape, there's no doubt about that, but I think it's a little disrespectful." Of course, I didn't understand what he was talking about; the jokes in Chalk Talk are squeaky clean. "Well," the patient said. "I take my Catholicism

very seriously, and I don't think it's very funny to
dress a comedian up as a priest."

In the spring of 1974, Father Martin was sent by the Navy to
speak to sailors stationed on Diego Garcia, a tiny island in the
Indian Ocean. The trip coincided with Holy Week and Easter
Sunday, and on Easter Monday, as soon as Father arrived on the
West Coast, he called home to say hello. Mae still remembers
how difficult it was for her to tell him that Austin Ripley had
died on the previous Thursday evening, April 11, 1974. Father
Martin was devastated. He was in California, unable to attend the
funeral of the man whom he loved and respected—and to whom
he owed his life. Father recalls that although he was overwhelmed
with grief and sorrow, he quickly realized that Austin Ripley had
died on Holy Thursday night.

> That's the night of the Last Supper, the night
> when Jesus Christ created the institution of the
> priesthood. I realized immediately that when Rip
> appeared before God to render an account of his
> life on earth, he had the lives of 1,500 priests—
> God's anointed—to pay as his price of admission.
> I knew at that moment that Rip was safe in God's
> hands.

Father Martin had never lost contact with his good friend.
From 1958 until the month of Ripley's death, they maintained a
regular correspondence, and Father managed, despite his increasingly busy schedule, to visit Guest House at least once a year, if
only for one night. In addition, every Christmas, Father sent a
donation to Guest House. The amount, Father recalls, "was always
less than I wished it could be."

Despite Father Martin's grief, he also felt some relief that his
good friend was no longer in pain. Toward the end, Ripley's life
had been filled with suffering and loss: he was blind the last three
years of his life, and he once described his blindness to Father as
"my heaviest cross." In addition, his wife, to whom he was devoted, was suffering from irreversible senility. In one of the last let-

ters Ripley wrote to Father Martin, dated June 2, 1973, he explained the circumstances that he and Lee were enduring:

> I think I told you I went to Chicago—my dear friend, Johnny Sheils, drove me down—to consult a noted ophthalmologist there, a good friend and a fine A.A. After a most thorough examination he advised that my optic nerve was dead, hence there was no chance of restoring sight to my right eye. [Ripley had already lost the sight in his left eye.] This was most shocking and shattering. But I continue to investigate other possible sources of help. Principally relying on the absolute faith and the compassionate mercy of God to restore my sight.
>
> Lee's sister took her to Rochester, Mayo Clinic, about ten days ago. After a thorough series of examinations they advised that there was absolutely nothing they could do to improve her condition! I am really far more concerned with her deplorable and pitiable situation than I am in the restoration of my sight. But here again I rely in utter faith upon the power of God to improve her condition.

Neither Austin nor Lee Ripley's conditions improved; in fact, they deteriorated quickly. However, until the last week of his life, Austin Ripley had devoted every waking hour to the project he had begun four years earlier: establishing a recovery facility for alcoholic nuns modeled on Guest House.

At Austin Ripley's funeral, held in Menomonie, Wisconsin (where Ripley had spent his final years), Father Philip Donnelly, a Jesuit priest who had met Ripley at Guest House and who had become his close friend, said:

> In all my years of priestly experience and of life, I have never met a man who more embodied the program of our Lord and Savior Jesus Christ than Austin Ripley.... What he did for all of us who

are graduates of Guest House was, together with his deep penetrating knowledge of the disease, to show love and compassion such as most of us had never experienced in our lives. What motivated him? It was the spirit of being sent. It was a deep realization of the faith expressed in his primary virtue which is gratitude, and he realized deeply that he had been gifted by God with all these natural talents, only to submerge them and let them be absorbed like the infinite love that had called him forth from the living slavery of alcoholism, to give to others what he had received.

Father Martin continued to give credit to Austin Ripley for everything he knew about alcoholism, but now, he did so in the past tense. "I'll never stop thanking him," Father notes. "He is in my daily prayers, especially during my thanksgiving after communion."

Father Martin's fame had begun to spread even more quickly and steadily as a result of the success of his Chalk Talk. More and more often, as he walked through airports or hotel lobbies, people would recognize him, introduce themselves, and explain the effect that hearing him talk or seeing his tapes had on their recovery. Often, they would ask for his autograph. Each time this happened, Father Martin was gracious, friendly, and sincerely interested in what the person had to say.

A pattern began to develop as Father became better known. People would line up after his talks. Then, one by one, they would mention the location where they had first heard him speak, along with the year and a particular detail. The result was a litany of grateful and sincere voices that often moved Father to tears:

> I haven't had a drink since Buffalo, 1968;
> I heard you in Pittsburgh in 1973 and you saved
>   my marriage;
> Thank you for Baltimore, 1960;

143

> I had my last drink the day I heard you in Washington, D.C., in 1971;
>
> I got my children back last year after two years of sobriety;
>
> You saved my life, Father; I'll never forget you.

Father Martin made eye contact with each speaker; often, he would embrace the person he was speaking with, and he would bellow a hearty and sincere congratulations if someone had just celebrated an anniversary of sobriety. Father never seemed to grow tired at these times; in fact, they seemed to invigorate him.

People often ask Father how he manages to deliver the Chalk Talk so often—sometimes three or four times in one week—without getting bored. Father explains:

> Every time I give the Chalk Talk, I hear Doc Green's voice, and each time, some truth gets nailed down a bit more deeply into my consciousness. I learned from the Jesuits at Loyola High School and at Loyola College their philosophy of education: "Repetition is the mother of learning." No one wants a surgeon standing over him saying, "Wow, I'm really excited to be doing this surgery for the first time." Instead, you want a surgeon who has performed the same operation many times. It is the repetition that ensures competence and success. As a priest, many of the actions I perform are repetitive, but it is through repetition that I develop a deeper understanding of what I am doing and a greater ability to do it well.
>
> The last thing in the world the people who come to hear me speak need is to hear me try something new, just for the excitement of it. They want and deserve to hear something that I have worked on, practiced, and delivered so many times that I will be at my best and give my best.

Father Martin's growing fame in the field of alcoholism had little if any impact on his personality or ego. In fact, even today, although he is one of the most renowned and revered figures in the field, he still insists that he deserves no credit for his work, claiming again and again that he is simply repeating what he has learned from Austin Ripley, Dr. Walter Green, and all of the others. "I like to boast," Father often says, "that I got my sobriety second-hand from the founders, Bill and Doctor Bob, through Austin Ripley."

When people thank Father for what he had done for them, he tells them that they are the ones who deserve his thanks, for he discovered long ago that contributing to an alcoholic's recovery provides more fulfillment and happiness than anyone could ever imagine.

Father's sense of humor has also helped him to cope with his growing fame. "If you think my job doesn't have its drawbacks," he likes to say, "just put on a Roman collar and get on a train."

> You'll be sitting there, just minding your own business, maybe praying or reading, and suddenly from the other end of the car you hear it: "HEY FATHER." Of course, you keep your head way down, stick it as far into your newspaper or book as you can, and just pray to the good Lord that the voice and its owner will go away. But deep in your heart you know it won't. "I'M A CATHOLIC."
>
> Now that everyone in your car has just learned that the guy who has had way too much to drink is a Catholic, they start to look in the direction of the person he's screaming at. You know you can't hide behind your newspaper forever, so you lower it slowly, smile at the guy who's staggering toward you, slide over in your seat so that he doesn't land in your lap, and get ready to hear his life story.

Living with the Abraham family also helps Father to keep his balance. Even if his sense of self-importance gets a bit inflated as a result of visiting foreign countries, meeting prominent people, eating in the best restaurants, receiving standing ovations, it would quickly be brought down to size as soon as he got home: when Alex was younger, he would try to guess how much weight Father had gained on his latest trip. (When Father is on the road, out of Mae's sight, he tends to indulge his fondness for desserts.) Alex could never bear the thought of hurting Father's feelings, however. He once used part of his allowance to buy Father a small statue of an overweight man standing on a scale trying to peer over his stomach to see his weight. At the bottom of the statue, a small plaque reads, "I like you just the way you are." (Father so treasured this gift that today, more than 30 years later, it is on the dresser in his bedroom.)

Mae probably understood Father Martin better than anyone else, and she eventually began to realize the reason Father was able to remain so unaffected by his success: "He always got more than he gave when dealing with alcoholics." Mae remembers one occasion in particular when he called from Miami after giving a talk at a dinner there. He told her about a man who came up to him afterward and said, "My name is Bruce Green. I'm Doc Green's son." Father was so delighted to meet the son of the man who had meant so much to him that they spoke at length about Bruce's dad, about Guest House, and of course, about Austin Ripley. They also talked about the fact that Dr. Green had converted to Catholicism shortly before his death, primarily as a result of the time he had spent with the priests at Guest House.

Mae recalls that when Father came home, he was so excited that he couldn't stop talking about it. "Can you imagine, Mae," Father kept saying, "meeting Doc Green's son. What a thrill." Mae remembers the joy that Father felt at the thought of Dr. Green's conversion. "The priests were able to give him something back for all he gave us," Father said.

Father Martin believes that the primary reason he is able to remain unaffected by the recognition and praise is because of Mae Abraham. "Mae was and is a true friend to me," Father recalls.

She is proud of my work, but as one who really cares about me, she also offers criticism or advice if needed. I accept this with gratitude and act on it, because I know it is given with love to make me grow and be better. If she says that something needs correcting, there is no arguing—it needs correcting.

In 1978 Father Martin and Mae accepted an invitation to speak at Fellowship by the Sea, an annual gathering of more than 3,000 alcoholics and their families in Myrtle Beach, South Carolina. By this time, Mae had heard Father speak many times, but she still remembers her reaction and the reaction of the others to the talk he gave that evening.

Father began, as always, with several jokes. Then, he began to talk to the people who had gathered there from all over the United States, and suddenly I was transported back to the first evening I had heard him at Johns Hopkins University. He spoke about our disease with humor, intelligence, and dignity. And I was reminded of the gift he had given me: the gift of knowledge about my disease, and as a result, the gift of sobriety.

When Father finished, he received a standing ovation, and as I looked around the room, I saw that some people were crying. Father was always effective, but that night, he was magnificent. He was with other alcoholics on that occasion, probably the largest gathering of alcoholics that he had ever addressed, and he seemed to be inspired to speak even more eloquently. I was crying as well, and I suddenly realized that Father Martin was probably the best speaker about alcoholism anywhere. He possessed a great gift, and I and the other people in that huge hall all seemed to be aware of it at that moment.

Mae was quiet on the way to the airport, but when she and Father were finally settled and the plane had taken off, she tried to explain what she had felt that night. "Father, you can talk until you die," she said, "but then what? Why don't we build a treatment center where everything you stand for can go on, where laypeople can get the kind of treatment priests got from Rip at Guest House?"

Father remembers that he was "immediately excited by the idea," and he asked Mae where they could build such a place. Mae replied: "Our family farm in West Jefferson, North Carolina, has sat vacant for nine years. I believe my family would gladly let us use it." When Father asked about funding, Father remembers that Mae responded: "the Good Lord will help us raise it." Father still remembers his response:

> I thought for about ten seconds and then told Mae that it sounded like a wonderful idea. Why not? My teaching days were over, and I was completely committed to helping alcoholics by that time. Every morning in my prayers, I thanked God for letting me share my gift of sobriety with others.
>
> People still ask me if I knew what I was getting myself into; after all, it took us seven years to fulfill our dream. But what people didn't understand is that I was dealing with Mae Abraham. The woman is absolutely fearless about unknown shores. And from the moment she entered my life, good things happened to me. I never even questioned the wisdom or the practicality of her suggestion—if Mae thought it was something worth pursuing, that was good enough for me.

CHAPTER SIX

Ashley: The Possible Dream

*A*lthough Father Martin and Mae Abraham were each aware of the other's extraordinary devotion to alcoholics, their decision to work together to establish a treatment center was still remarkable: Neither Mae nor Father had any experience in fund raising, in obtaining the necessary legal permits and licenses, in professional counseling, or in the technical aspects of running a treatment center. Although Tommy Abraham had been successful in his restaurant business and later in a car dealership that he established, enabling Father, Mae, and Alex to live comfortably, they were not wealthy, nor did they have connections with wealthy or influential people.

Mae and Father were concerned about these matters, of course, but they were not deterred. Mae had realized that Father was making one of the most important contributions in the world to the recovery of alcoholics, and she was determined to find a way for his work and influence to continue. Father had realized that Mae's devotion to the recovery of alcoholics was so deep and genuine that establishing a treatment center was an almost inevitable next step in the work she had been doing during her years of sobriety. "By this time, Mae's impact had been felt by practically every recovering alcoholic in the county," Father recalls, "and she was the one who inspired everything we did to help recovering alcoholics."

Tommy Abraham was also willing to do everything he could to help. By this time, he recalls, "The three of us had grown so close, and I had developed such a respect for the way recovering alcoholics helped each other, that I was as caught up in the project as they were." Furthermore, Tommy reasoned,

> Very few weeks went by when Mae wasn't working with some woman alcoholic new to sobriety. Mae's sisters and brothers had nicknamed them "Mae's lost souls." I saw the way that Mae treated these women, with extraordinary dignity, patience, and respect. And more often than not, as a result of Mae's care, they began to get well. So I knew that if there was anyone who had the talent and the desire to open a place where people could recover with dignity and respect, it was Mae.
>
> Father was known everywhere for his Chalk Talk and for his integrity, so the moment people learned that Father Martin was involved in the project, they responded with enthusiasm and confidence.

While it was true that Father and Mae had no practical experience in running a facility, they knew what proper treatment should be. They had a vision, the same one that had guided Austin Ripley through his years of struggle to open Guest House. Borrowing from the philosophy of Guest House, Ashley would be "a hospital and a hospice, a haven and a sanctuary" where "each patient shall be treated as priceless in the eyes of God."

During these early days of planning and discussion, Father would remember advice Ripley had passed on to him from Bill Wilson: "The good is too often the enemy of the best. Those who settle for what is good have settled, so the good can then become a barrier against reaching for the best." As a result, Father resolved that everything about Ashley, from the physical location to every aspect of care, would be of the highest possible quality. "What we wanted," Father recalls, "was the best atmosphere in which shattered alcoholics could get well."

Mae had her own reasons for agreeing with Father's philosophy. During the early days of her own sobriety, there were very few recovering women in her local group, making her feel isolated and somehow "deficient and different," and furthermore, society seemed to attach a far greater stigma to women who drank.

> I was made to feel worthless; my actions were viewed as bad and sinful. People would actually say that as a wife and mother I should be ashamed of myself for drinking and behaving that way. As a result, I envisioned a place where people could begin to heal, not only from the disease, but from the way that society had treated them. There would be no finger pointing, no blaming, no judging—only kindness, understanding, and knowledge.

Everyone who remembers Mae and Father during this early planning stage agrees that neither of them could have embarked upon such an ambitious project alone; but together, they had the determination they would need to proceed. "Father had the vision as a result of his experience at Guest House and as a result of having met and helped so many people through his talks and films, which had become part of the therapy of most treatment centers," Tommy recalls. "And Mae was the practical one. Their enthusiasm was so contagious that everyone they spoke to began to offer help."

Actually, the offers of help were a result not only of their enthusiasm, but also of the goodwill their actions on behalf of alcoholics had engendered over the years. Given the reputation that Father and Mae had earned in the community as a result of their work, there were many people, not only recovering alcoholics, but also grateful family members and friends of alcoholics, who were willing to help in any way they could. However, the fact remained that Father and Mae still had to ask for help: "No matter how you look at it," Father recalls, "we were begging for funds, and that's never easy."

Father Martin remembers that once word of their idea began to be known, people would come up to him after he had given a talk and hand him small donations.

> I remember one woman in particular who, for many years, sent me a check every month for five dollars, writing: "That's what I used to spend on a fifth of whiskey; now I'd like it to be used to help others." It was at moments like that when I knew we had to make it.
>
> Furthermore, knowing that we already had the Ashley property on which to build our center really helped us to get focused; it made it easier to describe our project to potential donors.

Mae and her sister, Mary, had been the first members of their family to move from West Jefferson, North Carolina, to the Aberdeen area of Maryland during World War II. However, over the years, Mae's parents and several of her brothers and sisters had also moved north, leaving the 54 acres of farmland that the family owned unused. The mountains of North Carolina are glorious, and the Ashley family land was on the side of one of these mountains; trails ran along beautiful stands of trees and wild grasses, and there was a large, crystal-clear lake on the property.

Mae's sisters and brothers consented immediately to her plan to build a center for the treatment of addicted people on the family land, and they were deeply honored when Mae and Father informed them that they had decided to name the facility Ashley in honor of their parents, Molly, who had died in 1963, and Arthur, who had died in 1975.

Although Mae and Father realized the advantage of owning the land on which they would build, their task was still enormous: they could use the proceeds from the videotapes and lectures to pay the expenses involved in traveling around the country to raise money, but they were certainly in no financial condition to begin building.

Father Martin still remembers the day Mae came home from the library with a thick book under her arm. "It contained the names of all the foundations in the country, and Mae was deter-mined to contact those that might help," Father recalls. "Neither of us had ever written a grant proposal before, but that didn't stop Mae. She was indefatigable, as always." Father remembers that Mae hired an architect to draw up preliminary plans, and he placed the cost of building a facility on the North Carolina prop-erty at about five million dollars. Father remembers that he "about passed out" when he heard that sum, but Mae assured him, with her usual good sense and poise, that he shouldn't be so worried; it wasn't as if they needed all of the money at once. "That seemed to make some sense," Father recalls. "Not a lot, but some."

Father and Mae decided that they would give a name to their plan, and they coined the phrase, "Ashley: The Possible Dream," using it in mailings, brochures, speeches, and proposals. However, Father Martin soon began to joke that perhaps they should add the subtitle "Seven Years of Begging."

Austin Ripley and Dr. Green had taught Father Martin that one aspect of true wisdom is knowing what you don't know. Father Martin recalls,

> It's being willing to ask for help. And Mae was very wise. She knew that we knew very little about the legal and financial aspects of our proj-ect, and so she asked for advice and assistance. Some of Ashley's best friends were made that way—by Mae calling and asking for answers to her questions. She never exhibited pride or arro-gance; she never pretended; she never bluffed; she never had to be the one in control or the one making the decisions. And people were so impressed by her honesty and modesty that they would do anything for her.
>
> One of the first "friends" that we made this way was Hal Tulley. A friend of a friend put us in touch with him; he was a lawyer from Bel Air, a suburb of Baltimore not far from the Abraham

house in Havre de Grace. Hal played a key role in the "birthing" of Ashley.

Ironically, the moment Father Martin heard the lawyer's name, he remembered having had a student at St. Charles College almost ten years before with the same name. "But it would be too much of a coincidence," Father recalls. "It was just a thought." However, when Father, Mae, and Tommy arrived at Tulley's office, they discovered that in fact, it was the same person; Tulley had left the seminary in 1962 and had subsequently become a lawyer.

Hal still remembers his amazement when Father Martin recalled, in precise detail, a short story that he had written as an assignment for English class in his fourth year of high school.

> It was a tale about a gunslinger. Father recalled that story to me in minute detail at the beginning of our first meeting—it just shocked me that someone would remember something like that after ten years.
>
> I later realized that Father had a wonderful trait that would endear him to everyone: he truly cared about people, what they did, what they had to say, and as a result, he often remembered much of what they told him.
>
> I was certainly glad to see him again, and it didn't take very long before I was entirely sold on their plan. I am not an alcoholic, but I was drawn to these good people who had very little to go on but knowledge, energy, enthusiasm, and trust in God. I was determined to help them in any way I could.
>
> Mae was very concerned about paying me for my services. I was married with young children, and she kept asking me when I would bill them. I later discovered that she was using much of her own money, but she never told anyone that. She just pretended that this was a very professional

business arrangement. I kept telling Mae that I would send the bill in due time, but as always with such relationships, I was getting so much satisfaction from helping these wonderful people and from being with Father Martin again after having had him as a teacher that I resolved to stick with them no matter what.

I guess that although I had left the seminary, I still retained the desire to help others, and I began to thrive on the legal challenge: we were dealing with the state of North Carolina by this time, trying to obtain permission to establish a facility, and soon after that we were trying to obtain tax-exempt status from the IRS, a task that would take us a full year.

As a result, I began to spend a lot of time in North Carolina, and that was my first introduction to real southern hospitality. Although people think that the early days of the project were all work and no play, I had some of the best times of my life with Mae's family. Mae's brother, Junior, owned a restaurant in West Jefferson, as did her sister, Mary, and I still remember, almost 30 years later, the biscuits and gravy and country ham. We were never allowed to pay a cent; Junior and Mary were insulted if we even offered.

We practically lived in their restaurants during those early days, and while the rest of us ate or prepared for meetings, Mae's other brother, Claude, and Father Martin would exchange jokes and stories. Claude had a strong southern accent, and Father, a great mimic, would out of the blue begin to talk just like Claude—it was amazing how accurately he captured the inflections of Claude's speech. But it was all so good natured and funny that Claude enjoyed it as much as we did.

155

Very often, Father Martin would be the first Catholic that some of the customers and workers in the restaurant had ever met, and he'd win them over with his sincerity and humor in no time at all. He told jokes, and he'd get to know the people. West Jefferson was Ashley country; people still remembered Mae's father, whom they referred to as the Reverend Ashley with great affection and respect; that also helped us to feel welcome and wanted.

All the southern hospitality in the world could not help Father Martin and Mae with some of the legal complications that were beginning to develop, however. In addition to trying to secure tax-exempt status, Mae and Father were informed that the state of North Carolina required them to obtain a "certificate of need" in order to establish such a treatment facility. Furthermore, unless construction began within a year after the certificate was granted, it would be rescinded. Mae and Father procured letters from experts in the field of alcoholism recovery to support their application; Conway Hunter, along with many others, wrote to the state board explaining not only the need for a facility but the expertise and devotion that Mae and Father would bring to such a project.

Hal still remembers all-night sessions trying to get paperwork completed in time to meet a deadline, only to discover that there were other rules and regulations that had to be dealt with. "Father may have grown a bit weary at this time," Hal Tulley recalls, "but Mae just kept saying that God would provide. She was always right of course, but everyone except Mae had doubts."

Shortly before Father and Mae obtained tax-exempt status from the I.R.S. for the project, Father had an opportunity to meet Sam Noble, a businessman from Oklahoma who had parlayed the already successful oil business he had inherited from his father into an even more successful enterprise. Sam Noble was as interested in giving money away as he was in earning it, so he used a family foundation that had been set up by his father to grant money to worthy causes. (In fact, the Noble Family was one of the University of Oklahoma's most generous donors.)

For Sam Noble, there was no cause more worthy than helping alcoholics to recover—a lesson he had learned as a result of the struggle his wife, Mary Jane Noble, had endured. Mrs. Noble had attempted recovery several times when she and her husband finally decided she should go to Alina Lodge, a treatment center in Blairstown, New Jersey, and Sam Noble spent time there participating in a family program. While at Alina, he and his wife saw several of Father's films, and Mary Jane remembers the effect they had on her husband (whom she called Bud).

> Bud was an intelligent and pragmatic business-man, yet he exhibited nothing but patience and compassion for me—doing everything he could to help me recover. When he saw Father Martin's videos, he suddenly realized that this man combined pragmatism with compassion. "This is a disease," Father would say, "and we must do everything we can to restore its victims through understanding and proper care."

Soon after Mary Jane Noble's recovery at Alina Lodge, the Reverend Richard Virtue, an Episcopal priest with whom Father had become friends, invited Father to speak at a fund-raising dinner in Norman, Oklahoma, in 1976 for the local Council on Alcoholism. Sam Noble, a member of Father Virtue's board at the Council, was at the dinner and heard Father speak. ("I'm convinced this is just one more of the many signs of Divine Providence that occurred throughout the seven years we were trying to raise funds and start Ashley," notes Father Martin.) After dinner, Father began to talk about the plans he and Mae had to start their own treatment facility, and although Sam Noble said little at the time, he was impressed by what Father had to say. "Bud saw a compassion in Father that he had never seen in any of the professionals with whom we had dealt throughout my

157

years of drinking," Mary Jane Noble recalls. "Bud's respect and fondness for Father was immediate and deep."

Not long after Father and Mae were granted tax-exempt status, Dick Virtue suggested that Father contact Sam Noble. Father recalls Dick Virtue's exact words: "This man could help you." And Father recalls the way that he proceeded:

> I had heard that Sam Noble was available to everyone, so I just picked up the phone, dialed his number, and he answered. I said, "Mr. Noble, this is Father Martin; I called to let you to know that we were granted tax-exempt status for Ashley." Sam Noble said, in a very kind voice, "Well, that's just great." He then went on to describe a "little building project" of his own: trying to build a place for the local A.A. and Al-Anon groups in his town to hold their meetings, and he said that he hoped they would be granted tax-exempt status, too.
>
> I was stumped as to what to say next. I just didn't have the nerve to say to this man, whom I'd met only twice, "We need money. Can you help us?" So I blurted out, "We need your advice." Sam Noble was his usual kind, efficient self, and he said, "Well, it may not be good, but it will be free. Why don't you and Mae come on out here to Ardmore and we'll talk about it." And that's exactly what Mae, Alex, and I did.

Initially, Mae and Father felt a bit intimidated by the Nobles' reputation as one of the most wealthy and prominent families in Oklahoma, but "Sam made us feel comfortable immediately," Father recalls.

> He met us at the airport, drove us to his home, and grilled steaks for dinner. As we ate, he asked us about our plans. He was a good listener, but he was also a good businessman, and he asked a lot of questions. By the end of the evening, he said that

he would arrange for our proposal to be placed on the agenda of his Foundation in the spring.

In March, he called telling us where to be and when. We arrived in due time, and I'm not sure who was more nervous, Mae or me. There were other people there to make presentations, and of course that made us a bit more jittery. We had prepared thoroughly, and we knew we had to be brief. It was one of the few times in my life I was scared. I had given the Chalk Talk thousands of times, but I had never asked anyone for a dime, and now I was about to stand before a seven-member board and try to sell them on making our "possible dream" real.

A few moments before we were scheduled to address the board, Sam came out of the meeting room and said, "Look, don't be nervous; these are nice people. Just be brief; state your facts; and don't ask for any given amount. Just tell them you'll be grateful for whatever they do." We went in, and I spoke for more than 20 minutes, and the board members seemed interested.

In fact, they were as taken with Father Martin as the thousands of other people who had heard him speak over the previous 20 years had been. His eloquence, his conviction, and his devotion to the recovery of alcoholics were evident that day. He talked about Austin Ripley and Dr. Green; he talked about Mae, and he talked about the need for a place where people would be treated with respect for their human dignity.

Father and Mae returned to Maryland, and the next evening, Sam himself called and told them that the board had agreed on a four-to-one matching grant: if Mae and Father could raise four million dollars, the Foundation would give them one million.

In addition, the Foundation would send a check for ten thousand dollars to use for travel and other expenses to raise the other four million dollars. Sam Noble told Father Martin that one of the board members was familiar with the area in West Jefferson where he and Mae intended to build, and the board member agreed that it was, in fact, one of "the most beautiful spots on earth." Mae was extremely pleased when she heard this; it was a confirmation of her deepest-held belief that only the best would be good enough for the treatment and recovery of people suffering from addiction.

It was at this time that Father asked Sam if he and Mary Jane would be willing to travel to Michigan to see the original Guest House and then to Minnesota where a second Guest House had recently been established. He wanted them to get a feel for what he had experienced and to see, first-hand, what proper treatment should be. Father remembers that they accepted "with eagerness and real enthusiasm." "By this time," Mary Jane Noble recalls,

> Bud had already developed a deep affection for Father. In fact, he had begun to call him Father Joe, although everyone else—except for immediate family and fellow priests—called him Father Martin. But Father welcomed the closeness and friendship. Furthermore, he recognized immediately that Bud's business and financial experience would be invaluable to him and Mae.
>
> Father was aware that he could speak well, but he knew nothing about business and finance. He came to rely on Bud more and more for advice, and Bud became more and more willing to give it. Bud was so busy at this time that I remember wondering where he would find the time to help with this project, but it wasn't work for him, it was almost a form of relaxation. Everyone felt that way when they were with Father.
>
> We enjoyed the visits to the two facilities, but as we listened to Father and Mae, we realized that their facility would eclipse not only the two Guest Houses, but most of the other facilities in existence at that time. That's not to say the other

160

facilities weren't top-notch, but they weren't being conceived and planned by two of the most extraordinary people Bud and I had ever met.

Bud would often talk about the project after spending time with Mae and Father, and he would say that there was something special about the idea. Bud was as hard-headed a businessman as you could find, but he was convinced—all of us were—that God's hand was present in this project, and that all of us were simply playing our part.

Father and Mae were ebullient over Sam Noble's generous grant. "I decided that fund-raising was a snap," Father recalls. "All I had to do was meet four more people like Sam Noble and we'd be home free. Well, it would be a long time before we met anyone else even vaguely like Sam Noble, and Mae and I began the long, hard struggle to raise the matching funds."

Mae remembers that as she and Father worked to establish Ashley, "God continued to place friends in our path." They attended a conference on alcoholism in Atlanta soon after they received the grant from The Noble Foundation, and as Mae stood on line in the hotel waiting to register, she heard the man at the head of the line give his name to the clerk. "It was Jamie Carraway," Mae recalls,

and of course Father and I had heard of his work in the field of alcoholism; he was one of the most prominent and highly respected experts in the field. I walked up to him, introduced myself, and said "Father Martin and I need your help and advice." Jamie had heard of Father, of course, and Father and I had heard of Jamie's enthusiastic endorsement of Father's Chalk Talk when the Navy asked him to review it.

Jamie said he'd be glad to help, and although he was directing his own center in North Carolina, and although our project could be perceived in a way as competition, he was true to his word.

Father continued to deliver as many talks as he could during this period, in order to help alcoholics, of course, but also to earn money that could be used to match the Noble Foundation grant. His schedule was so busy that he still remembers touching down in Chicago four times in one week on his way to different talks.

While he was on one of these trips, Tommy Abraham's brother died suddenly and unexpectedly, and of course, Father wanted to be in Pittsburgh for the funeral. However, if he flew on a commercial airline, he would not arrive in time, so someone recommended that Mae call Charlie Oliver, an insurance executive in Aberdeen who owned his own plane and had a commercial pilot's license. Oliver, who subsequently began to fly Father to his speaking engagements, remembers that he knew nothing about alcoholism, and even less about the Catholic Church.

> When I first got involved with Father Martin, I remember wondering what a Catholic priest was doing talking about alcoholism. In fact, after we arrived at the airport, Father told me to find a place to relax and get some sleep, but I was curious about what he was doing, so I asked if I could go along. I honestly didn't know what to expect.
>
> Well, as you can imagine, after 15 minutes of listening to him and watching the reaction of the people in the audience, I quickly realized that I was in the presence of a man who could save lives with his words. No one in the audience moved, they were so intent on what he was saying. Although I am not an alcoholic, I remember feeling a sense of security and well-being just listening to this man; he knew how to live life, how to keep his priorities straight, and through his demeanor, his peacefulness, and cheerfulness, he helped us to see it, too.

From that moment on, I was committed. As I got to know Father and Mae better, I realized that although they always seemed happy and confident when talking to donors or officials in some state agency or another, they were actually babes in the woods. I'd listen to them talking en route to a speaking engagement or to meet some official who was responsible for giving them approval to build in North Carolina, and when I heard the problems and the red tape they were facing, I almost wanted to tell them to give up on this fantastic idea, go home, and enjoy life.

But they were so sincere, so committed, so happy to be doing what they were doing, that I finally got as worked up about it all as they were, and I began to help in any way I could. I charged them the bare minimum—just enough to cover my own costs, and I promised to be available whenever they needed me. I remember worrying about Father sometimes; he would push himself to exhaustion, delivering four or five lectures in one week. He and Mae had to raise four million dollars in order to get the Noble matching funds, and that number pressed so heavily on them that sometimes I could have cried watching them struggle. I remember how despondent they would be when they would hear from some foundation or another that their request for help had been denied. Often, the letter would encourage them to re-apply the next year, but Mae would just look at Father and say, "If we don't get the money now, there won't be a next year."

But there were good times as well. We were constantly flying in and out of North Carolina trying to get the officials there to approve our plan, and as we would approach the airport, the worry lines in Mae's face would disappear—she was home. We'd go to her brother's or her sister's restaurant, and we'd have so much fun at one place or the other, telling jokes and stories, eating good Southern food, feeling very much at home, that pretty soon everything would seem all right again.

I was considered a local celebrity because of something that had happened once when we landed at the West Jefferson airport. I looked over to my left and saw a huge two-engine prop plane on the runway. I knew immediately that a plane that large had no business landing at that airport, and that the pilot could not have gotten clearance from the tower, because there was no tower. I called over to the pilot who was still in the cockpit, but he wouldn't climb down to talk to me.

So I radioed the FBI in Baltimore, and the next thing we heard, the plane had been searched and confiscated—it was full of marijuana. Mae didn't think the story was amusing at all; she kept imagining what could have happened to us if the pilot had pulled a gun out. But Father loved that story.

Despite the help of good friends like Charlie Oliver and Hal Tulley, and despite Father and Mae's best efforts, after more than a year of driving themselves harder than they ever had before, they had been able to raise only five hundred thousand dollars for the Ashley fund, far short of the four million they needed in order to be entitled to the one million dollars Sam Noble had promised. Furthermore, because they had not broken ground within a year of the issuance of the Certificate of Need from the state of North Carolina, the certificate was rescinded, and they were back where they had started. Father Martin remembers the way he felt:

I was as close to quitting as I ever came, but Mae wouldn't let me give up. No way. She was scared and discouraged too, but she had to keep her fears to herself in order to keep the rest of us from giving up completely. When things are at their worst, Mae is at her best. You would never know from looking at her and listening to her that we had just lost a permit that we had worked almost two years to get, spending a lot of our money in the process, and that we needed to raise three and a half million dollars. She'd just get that determined look in her eyes and say in her soft voice, "Now, Father, you know that God will get us through this one. He always does."

As always, Mae was right. They explained their predicament to Sam Noble, and he arranged for the board of the Noble Foundation to change the matching grant from four-to-one to one-to-one. At this time, Sam Noble suggested that Mae and Father look for an existing building that could be converted into a treatment center.

The plan to build in West Jefferson, North Carolina, was falling through for another reason as well. Tommy Abraham had begun to realize that the location of the Ashley property—two hours from the nearest commercial airport in Charlotte—could be a potential problem; most of the successful treatment centers were within an hour or so from a major airport.

Father Martin remembers that one day, after he and Mae returned from a particularly exhausting trip to North Carolina, Tommy sat them both down and asked Mae, as gently as he could, if she would consider locating her facility anywhere else but on the land that belonged to her family. Mae indicated that, given the fact that the certificate had been rescinded, she would be willing to do whatever she had to if it meant that the project could go forward. Tommy then explained that he had been making inquiries right there in Maryland.

Alex, who had been only 14 years old when Father Martin moved into the Abraham house, had by this time completed school and was planning to get married and remain in Havre de Grace. Although Mae was utterly consumed with the Ashley

165

project, she was still very much a mother, and the idea of remaining close to her son and her future daughter-in-law—and any future grandchildren—was extremely appealing to her.

Tommy enlisted the help of Hal Tulley and Jamie Carraway to find a suitable location in Maryland, and Jamie Carraway still remembers one particular incident that occurred at about this time.

> Suddenly, I was in the real estate business. I remember looking at a duPont estate on the Eastern Shore of Maryland, but it proved unsuitable. The next thing I knew, Tommy asked me to look at the Chrysler estate, also on the Eastern Shore. The executors of the estate were going to sell off the buildings and auction off the contents. I liked what I saw, and the next thing I knew, I found myself in Manhattan sitting in the board room of Columbia Pictures negotiating to buy an estate that had belonged to the married daughter of Mr. Chrysler himself.
>
> I looked around the table, and I just laughed and said to myself, "Here I am, a drunk from North Carolina, wheeling and dealing with these Eastern establishment lawyers, accountants, and financial wizards. If only the folks back home could see me now." Unfortunately, we couldn't agree on a price, but that sure was an experience.

In 1982, after several months of searching, Father, Mae, and Tommy finally found the perfect location for their facility, and ironically, it was less than nine miles from their home. The estate, known as Oakington, was owned by the widow of Senator Millard Tydings and consisted of 380 acres. Although the mansion was stately and beautiful, it needed major—and very expensive—renovation. The 20 acres on which the mansion and the carriage house stood had become overgrown, but it was still one of the finest pieces of land in the area. Most important, it was waterfront property; the view of the Chesapeake Bay was incredible.

The estate has a long and fascinating history. Land records show that in 1659, an 800-acre tract of land was surveyed and registered as Oakington Farm to a British army officer, Colonel Nathaniel Ute, a gift from the King of England. In 1672, the estate was divided in two: 300 acres were transferred to Ruten Garrett and the remaining 500 acres were transferred to Thomas Brown, who paid for the land with 3,000 pounds of tobacco. (In fact, Thomas Brown's gravestone is located behind the carriage house.)

Land records indicate that in 1812 John Stump purchased the land and the stone mansion that had been built there to be used by his son, John Wilson Stump, and his bride-to-be. It is known that the property remained in the Stump family until 1865, but there is no further record of ownership for the land until 1895, when it was purchased by The Hunt Club. The estate became known as "The Blind," and it was used as an exclusive duck-shooting club.

Then in 1905, James Lawrence Breezy, a member of the club, purchased the property to be used for his private residence. He hired Stanford White, a personal friend, and at the time one of the most prominent (and eccentric) architects in the world, to improve the property. Under White's direction, a wing was added to the original mansion.

The next owner, Commodore Leonard Richards, a millionaire from Wilmington, Delaware, purchased the estate in 1915. He built the stone north wing, added the solarium, and oversaw major improvements to the land itself. After Richard's death in 1933, the estate was leased to a Major Enoch B. Garry, and for the next two years it was used as a private boys' school. Then in 1935 the estate was purchased by U.S. Senator Millard E. Tydings, who resided there for 44 years. Scores of prominent people, including governors, senators, and several presidents (including John F. Kennedy) visited the estate while Tydings lived there.

By the time Mae, Father, and Tommy decided to purchase the estate in 1982, the main building had deteriorated to such a degree that there were two feet of water in the basement. New windows would have to be installed, and the plumbing, heating, and electrical systems would have to be upgraded or replaced completely. The state of Maryland required that Father and Mae procure a certificate of need, just as North Carolina had. Before Ashley could open as a treatment center for alcoholics and drug addicts, county and state codes and laws would have to be met. In addition, a sprinkler system would have to be installed; exits would have to be installed or relocated; standards such as square foot per patient would have to be met.

Father, Mae, and Tommy realized that the repairs would be exceedingly expensive, on top of the million-dollar purchase price, but they also knew that the property was perfect for their needs. Tommy realized the advantage of the proximity of the estate not only to their home but also to the Philadelphia, Baltimore, and Washington, D.C., airports, each only an hour or so away, and Mae and Father knew that with the proper renovation, the estate would be the perfect location for Ashley. "Just looking over the Chesapeake Bay gives a sense of serenity," Mae recalls,

> and I knew right away that our patients would feel it as well. Father didn't say so at the time, we were so preoccupied with more pressing matters, but later, after we bought the place, he told me the very first time he stood on the property and looked out over the Bay, he knew where he would someday like a chapel to be built. In the meanwhile, he used the solarium to celebrate Mass.
>
> Furthermore, although everyone warned us that repairs would be expensive and time-consuming, Tommy had helped Father and me realize that having an existing building, no matter how much in need of repair it was, was far cheaper than constructing one. It would be a struggle, but we could afford the Tydings estate.

Hal Tulley continued to help Mae and Father, and because he had been practicing law for so many years in the area, he knew whom to call in order to keep the bureaucracy happy. "I knew that we would have to pay certain fees and get certain approvals," he recalls,

> but I wanted to get these things taken care of as quickly as possible. So I arranged for all of the agencies and inspectors to come to the estate on the same day and at the same time so that they could talk to one other. In that way, we wouldn't run into a situation where agencies were giving contradictory instructions or orders.
>
> It was actually rather humorous. I sincerely believe that no one had ever brought all of these folks together before, although they all worked for the state of Maryland, and they were amazed at the ease with which decisions were made. Tommy and I were staying on top of everything, taking notes and making sure we followed what was going on.
>
> Mae had only one thing on her mind: the mansion had a magnificent open staircase, and one of the inspectors had hinted that it would probably have to be closed in order to satisfy some safety code. Mae was determined to save that staircase no matter what it took. The place was filled with inspectors measuring, talking, jotting down notes, making phone calls to check with their supervisors, and all Mae cared about was that staircase. I think if she had to, she would have parked herself on the banister and refused to move in order to save it. In the end, the staircase remained untouched, but I remember thinking that I was glad I was on Mae's side, because she could be very tough when she had to be.

Father recalls that he and Mae had come to realize how much they needed their "expert" friends. During one particularly difficult period in the contract negotiations, Mae decided that they should not proceed until they explained the problem to Sam Noble and sought his help. In turn, Sam Noble called Joseph Tydings, who was conducting the negotiations for his mother, and suddenly, Father recalls, "the problem disappeared."

Mae, Father, and Tommy brought in a local builder named Henry Bahr to oversee the renovations. Bahr was known throughout the community for his sense of perfection and for his sense of fairness. Initially, Bahr estimated that the cost of renovating the main building would be about three hundred and fifty thousand dollars. (In the end, it cost almost five times that amount.) After closing on the Tydings estate, Father and Mae had nothing left of the Noble Foundation's million-dollar donation, but as usual, Mae was undaunted. She just kept saying that if they worked very hard telling people about their project, the money would come in.

It did not come in quickly enough, however. Henry Bahr still remembers the "juggling" that Mae was forced to do throughout the entire period of renovation.

> It was one of the biggest projects I had ever worked on; it took about 14 months. I had told Mae, Father, and Tommy that they were getting a good deal, and they were, but I also told them that they had to expect to pay a lot of money to get the place the way they wanted it. Mae insisted we do things right, no short cuts. She was on a mission to make that place beautiful for the patients, and none of us dared disagree with her.
>
> But we kept running into problems that we hadn't anticipated. For example, we discovered that under the laundry—the area we were redesigning to be used as the kitchen, there were several hand-dug wells that had long been abandoned. Snakes were nesting in those holes—now

170

that was quite a discovery. Of course, we had to fill the wells up with dirt and then pour about six feet of concrete on top.

That was just one of the unexpected expenses. The mansion had been built more than 100 years before, entirely by hand, and the stone walls were more than two feet thick. We had men on the site whose only job was to cut holes in the walls using air compressors and bits and chisels. It was excruciatingly slow work, and it would often hold up the other workers.

We had to build the septic tank field, and I still remember the day the bill came in for the stones—we used about fifty thousand dollars' worth of stone on that job. Father Martin wanted to know if the stones were made of gold.

We never actually had to stop work because of money, but there were some very close calls. I knew that Mae and Father were struggling, so during the last six months of construction, I told them I could wait for payment, but the subcontractors wanted to be paid on time. There were days when Mae's checkbook balance would be down to nothing, and nobody knew what she would do. I know that on those days, Mae would be on the phone calling potential donors, trying to raise enough money to keep the work going. She knew that if we had to stop, it would delay completion and put them in a worse financial bind.

I hardly knew Mae Abraham at the beginning of the project, but by the end, I had developed such respect for her that I would have done anything she asked me. In the midst of her own struggles, she would ask me, practically every day, if I was all right going without payment. "I know you have a family to take care of, Henry," she would say. "Don't go without. We can borrow the money if we have to." I'd tell her that I was perfectly fine, not to worry. And in the end, when their finances got a bit better, of course they paid me.

In fact, there was a point when Mae and Father had exhausted all of their options and were about to tell Henry Bahr to halt work. However, Father Martin recalls how, once again, "God intervened."

> I had come to know and become good friends with a successful businessman from Chicago named Russ Carpenter. When Russ died, his son, Bill, called Mae to say that his father had told him that he had bequeathed money to Ashley. However, Bill told me that because his sister was in New Zealand, the will would not be probated for quite a while. I was overcome with gratitude, of course, but when Mae and I realized that we were so short on funds that construction would have to stop, Mae suggested that I contact Bill and ask him for a letter of intent. In that way, we could perhaps get the bank to lend us some money using the inheritance as collateral. At the time, we believed the amount that Russ had bequeathed to Ashley was about $20,000.
>
> I was on my way home to get Bill's telephone number when a call came in for Mae. It was Bill saying that his father's will had been probated, and that he was on his way over to Ashley with a check for $75,000 in his hands, far more than we had expected. At that moment, our accountant walked into Mae's office and found her in tears of gratitude and relief. When I think of what that woman went through—it still amazes me.

Precisely one year elapsed from the time Ashley purchased the estate until it actually opened, and it was, Father recalls, the most exciting, frustrating, and challenging year of our lives. Nothing else mattered. Everything we did, we did for Ashley. Mae and I decided to increase my speaking fee and the number of lectures I gave to help with the Ashley restoration. Only the good Lord knows how much Tommy contributed; all I know is that one day there would be a bill due, and the next day Tommy would tell me not to worry, that it "had been taken care of."

But we were getting closer and closer, and there was no longer any doubt that we would make it. Mae and I had already put together a board of directors to help us. Of course we asked Hal Tulley; he had been one of our most loyal friends and he is a good lawyer. Mae and I had become good friends with Jamie Carraway, who had such experience and expertise from his years as executive director of Fellowship Hall, so of course we asked him to be on the board as well. Another good friend and board member was Christine Benati, a woman who cared very much about us and about our work, and who has never said no to any request we've made of her.

I had also become friends with Lou Bantle, who was at the time Chairman of UST in Greenwich, Connecticut. Five years earlier, I had told Mae that I doubted I would ever meet anyone as generous as Sam Noble, but I was wrong; Lou Bantle proved to be another of Ashley's most generous friends.

Mae and Father Martin asked Lou if he would be willing to serve on Ashley's board of directors, not only because of his business experience but also because of his deep knowledge and experience in the field of alcoholism. Lou's own recovery had begun years before he even heard of Father Martin. However, he had subsequently become Chair of the Southwestern Connecticut Alcohol Council, and in 1978, members of the council had invited Father Martin to speak as part of a fund-raiser they would be holding in Stamford, Connecticut. "Father and I became friends almost immediately," Lou Bantle recalls.

> I spent a whole day with him during that first visit, and it wasn't long before I realized the power of healing that Father Martin possesses. I'm not sure how to express this clearly, but Father Martin has the ability to make you feel good about being an alcoholic because he helps you understand the disease, and he helps you to regain your self-worth.

Lou Bantle accepted Mae and Father's invitation to join the board, and he decided to travel to Havre de Grace "to see what was going on." When he arrived, Mae and Father explained how precarious their financial situation was. Lou recalls that he turned to Mae and said, "Listen, this is a project that is going to help thousands of other suffering alcoholics, so you must not be ashamed of asking people for money."

Today, Lou and Mae still laugh when they recall the incident. "The only thing I had ever begged for in my life before then was a drink," Mae recalls. "And a lot of times, people refused me. But I've been taking Lou up on his advice ever since, and more often than not, people say yes."

"I created a monster," Lou Bantle notes. "Mae has become the consummate fund-raiser. Try saying no to her." (It would soon become apparent that Lou Bantle decided not to try—he has given Ashley more money than any other private or corporate donor, and UST, the company that he headed until his retirement in 1993, was equally generous.)

People who watched Father Martin and Mae work together were amazed by their ability to get along despite the fact that they were working brutally hard and that things very often did not work out in their favor. Everyone realized it was Mae's refusal to let anything get in the way that was going to result in the success of the project. "Mae tells me what to do," Father Martin became fond of saying at about this time. "I just follow her orders."

On one occasion, Jerry Herrera, a good friend who would later work at Ashley driving Father to his speaking engagements, was at the construction site with Father at the same time Lou Bantle was there. Lou had become concerned over Father Martin's weight. Worried about Father's health and aware that he gained most of his weight while traveling in order to raise funds for Ashley, Lou offered Father a thousand dollars for every pound he lost, up to 30 pounds. "I wouldn't make that offer in front of Mae," Jerry Herrera joked. "If she hears about it, I swear she'll whack Father's legs off."

Mae's sister, Camilla Thomas (whom everyone calls Micki), had begun to help Mae's other sister, Pat Hitchcock, who, in addition to her duties operating Kelly Productions, was getting more and more involved in fund-raising. Micki wanted nothing more than to help. "Mae saved my life," Micki recalls, "I would have done anything she asked me to do." Micki's alcoholism had taken a terrible toll on her life: Her marriage had failed, she had lost several jobs, and she had lost custody of her ten-year-old daughter. Family members and friends tried repeatedly to help, but within weeks, sometimes even days, Micki would again relapse until most people had given up any hope for recovery. "Not Mae," Micki recalls,

> she never gave up on me. I was a chronic relapser. I could get sober but I couldn't stay sober. People were tired of me; they wrote me off. Then one day in 1980, I found myself in a strange place, far away from friends and family, and I was sicker than I had ever been in my life. I realized that unless I got help immediately, I would die alone. I was in an alcohol-induced stupor, but luckily I was still able to make a phone call. I called Mae, but I was afraid that she, too, had given up on me.

She had rescued me so many times then I would turn around and drink again.

But Mae understood immediately how sick and desperate I was, and, as always, she came and brought me to her house, got me medical attention, sat with me for the first few nights after I returned from detox, prayed for me, never once saying that she needed to get back to Ashley, although I knew that's where she needed to be.

As Micki recovered, she began to help Pat and Mae with some of the paperwork in the small Kelly Productions offices in Aberdeen. Within months, as Micki's health and energy began to return, she was able to take more and more responsibility for arranging Father Martin's fund-raising trips. Micki had been a meeting coordinator for a medical and educational group before her drinking had gotten out of control, so she was perfectly suited for the task. "I remained behind the scenes, of course," Micki recalls,

> but I was so grateful for my sobriety and so grateful that people would trust me with any responsibility at all that I did everything I could to help Mae, Father, and Pat. We began to organize dinner and speaking engagements for Father around the country. We'd ask friends or people Father had met through his travels to sponsor a dinner or talk in their area, and arrange for Father to come and describe "Ashley: The Possible Dream."
>
> Pat and I oversaw all of the arrangements from our tiny office. We were working on top of each other, using boxes in which we shipped the tapes for file cabinets. Everything we mailed out looked professional with our "Ashley: the Possible Dream" logo, but in actuality we were always on the brink of disaster: understaffed, underfunded, trying to keep up with the Kelly Production side of the business while doing the fund-raising. Pat

was responsible for keeping the books and records straight for tax purposes; I still don't know how she managed to create order out of that chaos, but she did it with grace and humor. Fortunately, Mae's brother, Worth Ashley, and his wife, Helen, kept Mae's home going while Mae was consumed with her work at Ashley.

Father's reputation really helped our cause; more often than not, there would be a standing-room-only crowd, each of whom paid an admission fee to hear him. Afterward, he always called home to talk to Tommy and Mae, and he'd tell us how many people had attended. Based on that figure, Mae would be able to estimate how much she could give to Henry Bahr the next week to continue construction. Father was tired—we were sending him all over the country—but he never complained.

In fact, a list of partial donations from this period indicates that in the summer of 1982, as construction was nearing completion and funds were being depleted quickly, Father spoke in six cities in two weeks, raising $4,620 in Denver, Colorado; $11,653 in Newport Beach, California; $431.50 in Wilmington, Delaware (not enough to cover expenses); $5,556 in Gaylord, Michigan; $3,750 in Syracuse, New York; and $8,215 in Sioux City, Iowa.

Micki recalls that Father's popularity began to grow even more as a result of these presentations:

As word of his project began to spread, newspapers in the city or town where he was speaking would often run an article about his project. Some readers would send donations. These contributions would often move Father to tears. Sometimes the person wouldn't even write a check, just tuck a few dollars in an envelope with a little note blessing him and his work and wishing him luck. Father cherished those notes and responded to as many as he could, or he'd have one of us write if he didn't have the time.

There were many prominent businessmen in those audiences as well, and through them larger donations began to come in from corporations. Those donations, some of them as large as $50,000, would give Mae some peace of mind—she could then go for a day or two with some money in the checking account. But in the end, it was the thousands of small donations that made the difference. Ashley was built the hard way: one dollar at a time.

Although Mae and Father were consumed with the task of completing construction and beginning to plan for the day they would treat patients at Ashley, they never lost sight of what their work was all about. On one occasion, Mae was very late arriving at the construction site where Henry Bahr was waiting for her to make several important decisions before work could continue. But Mae had more important business to attend to first: she had spent an entire morning taking a young man in the early stages of recovery shopping for new clothes and shoes so that he would look presentable for a job interview she had set up for him that afternoon.

Father had maintained contact with Father Larry Taylor, the priest with whom he had developed a close friendship during his teaching days in California (and with whom he had his first martini). By the late 1970s, Father Taylor was no longer able to teach; in fact, he was barely able to walk as a result of the back injury he had suffered years before at the swimming pool at St. Joseph's College, and he was living in the Sulpician retirement home in Baltimore. Father Martin realized that Larry Taylor had few visitors, so as often as it could be arranged, Father and Mae would drive to Baltimore to bring his old friend to their home for a day. Father Taylor had recovered at Guest House several years after Father Martin did, and as a result, he too was enjoying sobriety. He was lonely however, and he looked forward to spending time

178

Father Martin with Father Larry Taylor, shortly before Father Taylor's death in 1980. (Courtesy of Father Martin.)

at the Abraham home. "Larry was as brilliant as ever," Father Martin recalls.

> We'd talk about all sorts of things, but as I would get ready to take him back, I would notice that he would grow quiet. I knew his life was a limited one because of his back injury. I remember once when I arrived I asked Larry what he had been doing. He smiled and said: "Waiting for you." I loved him, but his loneliness helped me realize two things: how important it was for me to visit him, and also how my alcoholism, my recovery, and meeting Mae had been a gift from God—I had a direction and a purpose for the rest of my life.

When Father Taylor died in 1980, Father Martin remembers feeling that he had lost one of the closest friends he had ever had. "I used to tease him about having introduced me to my first martini," Father recalls, "but he introduced me to many other things as well. He had a childlike devotion to Our Lady of Guadalupe, and he prayed for Ashley and us to her. I feel he's still interceding for us in heaven."

Father Martin, Mae and Tommy Abraham, with Alex's children, Tommy and Audrey Mae. (Courtesy of Mrs. Mae Abraham.)

Although Mae had no choice but to spend almost all of her waking hours at Ashley, she had two very good reasons to be distracted during the construction period: In 1981, her first grandchild was born, a boy, who was named Tommy after his grandfather. Then, in 1982, her second grandchild, a girl named Audrey Mae, was born. Mae and Tommy were thrilled, and they helped in any way they could: with gifts, with advice, and most important, with time. They baby-sat for the children whenever they were asked, and before long, there were cribs, playpens, blankets, toys, and children's books all over the house.

By late 1982, as construction neared completion, Ashley's board of directors began to plan for the day the first patients would be admitted; they even held a weekend retreat at which they reviewed their goals and priorities.

"Father and Mae were dying to get people into recovery," Lou Bantle recalls, "and while the rest of us were just as committed to helping alcoholics and drug addicts recover as they were, we were also pragmatic enough to know that we had to start generating income as quickly as possible."

The board made several other decisions during the weekend retreat as well. They realized that Father Martin's reputation was Ashley's greatest asset, so they voted to retain Mae's maiden name in honor of her parents, but to add Father's name as well. Thus, the documents of incorporation read "Father Martin's Ashley." Most people still refer to it simply as Ashley however, and as Father Martin says, "That suits me just fine." (Terry Gorski often jokes that although Father Martin's Ashley is a very beautiful and fitting name, the center should actually have been named "Chalk Talk University.")

Next, the board decided that Sam Noble needed to be recognized, not only for his generous financial donation, but for the advice he had given and concern he had exhibited over the past five years. Therefore, they agreed when Father and Mae decided to call the newly renovated mansion Noble Hall. Sam Noble was not in agreement with this, however; Mary Jane Noble recalls that her husband was uncomfortable with any form of recognition.

Neither Mae Abraham nor Father Martin would receive a salary from Ashley until three years later, when the board voted to place them on the payroll. "I guess we were just too busy to think about our own finances," Father recalls.

Father and Mae hired a director who would be responsible for the counseling staff and for overseeing the patients' treatment. "Mae and I knew what we could do well," Father recalls,

> but we were not about to try to replace professionals who had the proper training and credentials. I used to joke that I felt perfectly at home with a piece of chalk and a bunch of drunks. The rest of the technical stuff we'd leave to trained professionals. I was only half kidding. Mae and I had the vision, but we knew that only a staff with the best training and extensive experience working with alcoholics could make that vision a reality.

Father and Mae were determined to hand pick their staff members, and they had maintained contact with Leonard Dahl, the man whom Father and Mae had helped during his early struggles with sobriety in the 1970s, and whom Father Martin describes as "one of the kindest, gentlest, and most able men in the field." Father Martin had been invited to address a large group of recovering alcoholics in Pittsburgh at the tenth-anniversary dinner for Gateway, the facility where Leonard was working. Father and Mae talked about the possibility of asking Leonard to join the staff of Ashley, and they decided that the best time to do so would be when Father saw Leonard in Pittsburgh.

However, Father knew that Leonard was employed by another treatment center, and he and Mae realized that they had to be very careful not to "pirate" employees from other facilities simply to staff their own. Therefore, when Father asked Leonard if he ever thought of returning to Baltimore and he replied, "Not really," Father dropped the topic immediately.

Leonard still remembers the evening Father Martin spoke, "as if it were yesterday," and the effect that hearing Father had on him.

> There was a huge crowd gathered in the William Penn Hotel to celebrate the tenth anniversary of Gateway—more than 3,000 people—and I knew, based on my experience in the field of alcoholism recovery, that they had come primarily to hear Father. There were two very well known and highly respected athletes speaking that night, yet it was Father Martin that people wanted to see. When Father arrived, it was bitterly cold, yet almost 100 people were waiting outside trying to say hello to him, to touch him, to get his autograph. Father was as gracious as ever, ignoring the cold, listening and talking, not even realizing that the crowd wanted to see him when two of the most popular athletes of the day were there as well.

182

After Father's lecture, I drove him back to the airport, and we talked about the opening of Ashley. This must have been late in 1982, just a few months before the official opening, and I remember thinking to myself that Ashley would be a very special place—that the field of alcoholism recovery would truly be blessed by its existence.

When I got home that evening, I decided that I would like nothing better than to be affiliated with such a place, to have the opportunity to work with Father and Mae. So the very next morning, I wrote a letter to Father Martin asking if there were any openings at Ashley for a family therapist, since I had many years of experience in family counseling. Father called me when he received my letter and told me how he had actually tried to offer me a job. We laughed about the incident, of course, but I sincerely believe that God had a lot to do with the way things worked out.

Father Martin, Tommy, and Mae realized the value of having people at Ashley they knew and trusted. "We already had a core staff of competent and dedicated people whom we knew and loved," Father recalls. "When Pat and Micki agreed to continue to help us, Mae and I knew how lucky we were." In fact, all of Mae's family continued to help in any way they could, and Micki Thomas, at Mae and Father's urging, had begun to train under Jamie Carraway in a program that would enable her to earn the necessary credentials to work as a counselor at Ashley. Tommy Abraham had been devoting time to the project for more than seven years, and he would continue to oversee the financial end of the enterprise for several more years.

Father asked his sister, Marie, who had retired from nursing, if she would consider joining the staff of Ashley, and she immediately said yes. "Marie wasn't as young as she used to be," Father recalls, "and she only worked for us on a part-time basis, but she was strong, smart, and devoted to our cause. It was wonderful to have her around."

From the time that Mae had suggested to Father, almost eight years before, that they establish a place where his work could continue, Mae had worked tirelessly and fearlessly to make their dream a reality. As the date of completion grew closer, Mae worked even harder. "Everything had to be perfect or Mae wouldn't be satisfied," Father recalls.

> She drove herself so hard toward the end of 1982 that we all began to worry about her health. She was up earlier than anyone else and she went to bed after everyone else. Mae paid attention to every detail; nothing was too small. If you wanted to get a look from Mae that would freeze your heart, all you had to do was suggest that she was paying too much attention to the small details.
>
> Everything had to be perfect: the linen, the china, the carpets, the pictures on the walls. All of us, Mae's family, my family, board members, our friends and supporters, looked on in awe as Mae's "finishing touches" converted that big stone building into a home. We opened on Monday, January 17, 1983, a very cold day, but Noble Hall glowed with warmth. That feeling of warmth, comfort, and security wasn't coming from the new—and very expensive—heating system, however; it was coming directly from Mae Abraham, and everyone knew it.

CHAPTER SEVEN

※

Father Martin's Ashley

F ather Martin's Ashley opened its doors on Monday, January 17, 1983, with no fanfare. Of course, Mae and Father wanted to have an official dedication ceremony at which family, friends, and supporters could be present, but they decided to wait until the following fall. They were reluctant to hold a function for a large number of people in the dead of winter, but even more important, they wanted to concentrate all of their energies and resources on the patients themselves. "We knew there would be plenty of time to celebrate," Father Martin recalls. "Mae and I had to make the shift from planning a facility to running one, and we didn't want anything to interfere."

Leonard Dahl remembers that on opening day, five patients were admitted to Ashley. "We had six staff members and five patients," he recalls,

> and we later joked that we treated them like hot-house plants, hovering over them, worrying about them. We still remember their names. They were from different backgrounds, but they had a common bond in their alcoholism, and we had a common bond in our desire to help them get sober. Teachers often say that their first students are the most special and memorable to them; well, that was true for us at Ashley as well. I still have the first admission sheet with the names of those five patients on it. It's something we cherish.

185

Within the first two months of operation, the number of patients rose quickly, from five to 12, and then back down to four. Father and Mae began to worry, realizing that Ashley could not remain open unless something happened to increase their census. As always, they sought advice and help, this time from Jamie Carraway, who still remembers the phone call he received from them late one evening:

> Father told me that although the patients at Ashley were doing well, there just weren't enough of them. At the rate they were going they would not be able to stay open much longer. I was worried for them. I knew what Father and Mae had gone through to get Ashley started, and I heard the concern in his voice. He was beginning to realize the enormous responsibility he had, not only to the patients at Ashley, but also to the thousands of people who had contributed money and time to the project. Father was afraid that he might have to close Ashley for a while. I told Father not to do that; the risk was too great that it would not open again. My own company was doing well at the time, so I said, very emphatically, "Ashley will not close, not even for a day. I'll fly up tomorrow and we'll take it from there."

Within a day of his arrival, Jamie helped Mae and Father realize that their staff—which had grown to 17—would have to be reduced immediately. Next, at Jamie's suggestion, Mae, Tommy, and Father secured a personal loan from a local bank; they would use the money to keep Ashley running until the number of patients rose and stabilized. Again, Hal Tulley helped them, this time with the painful task of informing several staff members that they were being let go. "It was a difficult time for us," Father recalls.

Jamie Carraway then did something that was almost unheard of: he offered to provide Father and Mae with the day-to-day program that he had put into effect in his own successful facility,

Heritage Health, in Melbourne, Florida. "We were deeply touched by Jamie's generosity," Mae recalls.

> Can you imagine a competitor giving you the secret of his success? Well, in effect, that's what Jamie was doing. He had his assistant prepare a plan of activities for each of our patients and send it to us—it was a five-week schedule of around-the-clock activities. Jamie did not charge us for any of this. We were dumfounded at first by his goodness and generosity, knowing we could never be able to repay him, but we have come to know this is typical of the man.

During one visit, Jamie suggested to Father, in a rather matter-of-fact way, that Leonard Dahl be made executive director. Father was a bit confused since he and Mae had already hired a director, but Father soon began to realize the wisdom of Jamie's suggestion. Mae and Father had hired someone to direct the program at Ashley whom they believed had the best qualifications and experience, but within two or three months, they began to feel uncomfortable. "Mae and I never believed we were experts in the field of alcoholism recovery," Father recalls,

> so we looked to our new director for guidance in terms of setting up our program. But he didn't seem to be doing anything according to our philosophy of treatment. There was some counseling going on, but before Jamie helped us by providing us with the schedule in effect at his facility, our patients were being left with too many hours of free time. When I tried to talk to him about this, he would assure me that he knew what he was doing.
>
> Mae and I began to sense that Ashley was not becoming the place we had envisioned—it's hard to describe, but we didn't feel that sense of "community" that I had felt immediately at Guest House.

One day when I arrived home after spending the morning at Ashley, I realized that I had not been happy or comfortable being there. I asked myself what in heaven's name was going on. Mae and I had worked for seven years to establish a place where alcoholics and addicts would be made to feel comfortable and secure as they began to get well, and I myself didn't feel comfortable there. I remember telling Mae that we had a serious problem. We called Jamie Carraway, Sam Noble, and Hal Tulley, and they helped us to realize that there is no shame in making a mistake, but there is shame in not doing everything you can as quickly as possible to rectify it.

Mae and I had the director come to our home one Sunday morning and told him that we had to let him go. I explained the situation by using the term "no-fault divorce." We simply had different philosophies of treatment. The director (still a friend) accepted the news with good grace, and we were free to replace him with someone who shared our vision.

There was no question who that would be. We asked Leonard if he would assume the responsibilities of the directorship, and he accepted. I remember that he was deeply moved, and he told us later how gratified and honored he was by our expression of confidence. He's been our executive director ever since, and one of our best and most loyal friends.

Leonard, who had begun his work at Ashley as a therapist, acted immediately to implement Father and Mae's philosophy of treatment. No one could have been better qualified to do so. Leonard is an ordained Presbyterian minister (he earned his Master of Theology degree at Princeton) who shares Mae and Father's belief that the soul—as well as the body—needs nurtur-

Leonard Dahl and Mae Abraham, in one of the sitting rooms in Noble Hall.
(Courtesy of Mrs. Mae Abraham.)

ing and healing. Furthermore, soon after Leonard's own recovery,
he had begun training in the field, attending courses at the
Rutgers Summer School of Alcohol Studies, the Maryland
Institute of Alcohol Studies, and Washington College. In 1979 he
became a Certified Addictions Counselor, and in 1980 he attended the Johnson Institute in Minneapolis, Minnesota. He served
first as the executive director of the Mann House in Bel Air,
Maryland, a halfway house for alcoholic men, and then as a family therapist and pastoral counselor at Gateway in Pittsburgh.

Leonard Dahl was the perfect complement to Father and Mae.
Like them, he valued his own recovery and had decided to use
his experiences to help others, but he also possessed the professional training so essential to guiding Ashley as it developed into
one of the premier recovery centers in the United States.

One of Leonard's first decisions was to institute a family program at Ashley. Alcoholism is a family disease—it affects every
member of the family—and no one was more aware of this than
Leonard. In fact, several years earlier, when he decided that his
daughter, Elisabeth, was old enough to learn about the disease of
alcoholism, Leonard had taken her to hear Father's Chalk Talk. "I
wanted her to understand as much as possible about the disease,
and there was no one who could better explain it than Father
Martin," Leonard recalls.

I think every recovering alcoholic at some point becomes very concerned with the issue of who will explain this disease to the family, particularly the children, since there are so many misconceptions about it. So when Elisabeth began to ask me questions, I traveled from Pittsburgh, where I was working, to Baltimore, to bring her to hear Father speak one evening at Loyola College.

I wanted the families of the patients at Ashley to have the same opportunity that my daughter had, so an integral part of the family program was ensuring that every family member hear Father speak. His talks had an extraordinary effect on the family members. Many of them were learning about this disease for the first time, despite the fact that they had been living with it for years.

Father Martin, Mae, and Leonard quickly developed a wonderful working relationship: they communicated honestly and openly, with complete trust and confidence in each other; they put the welfare of their patients above everything else; and most important, they liked and respected each other. Leonard found himself included more and more often in dinner plans and in family gatherings at the Abraham house. Leonard and Alex became good friends, he soon got to know many of Mae's sisters and brothers, and he enjoyed Father Martin's family as well.

And more and more often, Leonard found himself enjoying Tommy Abraham's company. "Tommy had direct responsibility for the financial well-being of Ashley at the time," Leonard recalls, "so of course we discussed those matters all the time. But more and more frequently, Tommy and I would have lunch together; he was sensible, good natured, and easy to be with, and I came to value his friendship. I felt very much at home at Ashley."

The feeling was mutual. Everyone, especially the board members, quickly came to realize the crucial role that Leonard was

190

playing in Ashley's success. "He is the consummate professional," Lou Bantle recalls,

> and a most gentle and patient man. He complemented Father and Mae perfectly. Together, they provided leadership and vision for Ashley. As members of the board, we had always marveled at the way that Father and Mae worked together; now, whenever we talked about the success of Ashley, Leonard's name was mentioned along with theirs.
>
> Most of us on the board were businessmen, yet even with the expertise and resources at our disposal, we would never have been able to put such a team together—so as always, we simply shook our heads and concluded that God was the real director of Ashley.

Although the first several months were difficult for Father Martin and Mae, conditions at Ashley soon stabilized: as word of Ashley began to spread, more and more doctors, counselors, and other health professionals, as well as judges and lawyers, began to recommend Ashley. By June, Ashley was operating at its full capacity of 29 patients.

Father, Mae, and Leonard, with the extraordinary help of Jamie Carraway, had implemented—and then modified—a month-long program of recovery for their patients that included medical care, individual and group counseling, educational sessions, recreation, and family therapy. Every moment of the patients' day was accounted for.

More and more drug addicts were being recommended to Ashley for treatment, making the need for space even greater. Ashley did not discriminate against patients who suffered from drug addiction as well as from alcoholism. "I know that there were some who felt drug addicts should be treated separately," Father Martin recalls, "but I believed then, and I still believe, that the Twelve Steps of A.A. work for all addictions."

Ashley was beginning to be recommended in professional publications, and within two years of its opening, it was ranked in *Forbes* Magazine as one of the top ten facilities in the country, along with such illustrious institutions as Hazelden, which had been in operation since 1949, and the Betty Ford Center, which had opened in 1982. A description of Ashley that appeared in one of these professional journals chided the administration for spending money on such "amenities" as Oriental carpets, fine furnishings, a housekeeping staff, and outside maintenance. Mae was delighted with such criticism; she recalls:

> Father and I were well aware of other facilities where the patients' rooms were not so nicely furnished, where the patients were required to do chores, or where they were given "punishments" such as walking around with their pants on backwards, wearing signs advertising their faults, or having to sit in a "hot seat" while "confessing" details of their addiction. We had no intention of following that route. Our patients came to Ashley to recover from a disease, not to be punished for having a moral failing. As Father Martin always said, "The sickest of the sick deserve the best of care."
>
> I remember one particular woman, one of our early patients, who said she had never had anyone take care of her before, and she had never lived in such beautiful, clean surroundings, where her needs were taken care of. All she had to do, she said, was get well. I was so pleased to hear that.
>
> I explained to her my own experience in the early days of treatment, and I told her of my promise to myself when we first began to plan Ashley to make sure our patients were surrounded by beauty and comfort. "You've succeeded," the woman told me, "and you've succeeded in restoring my dignity as well."

Father Martin's Ashley had incorporated and implemented a highly successful professional model of treatment, and that model was supplemented and enhanced by the presence of Father Martin and Mae. "They were not absentee landlords. Their presence is what set Ashley apart from so many others," Jamie Carraway recalls. "The patients learned about the Twelve Steps through instruction, but they saw the Twelve Steps in action through Mae, Father, and the rest of the staff. Father was there, saying Mass each morning, and delivering the opening lecture five days a week."

Jamie Carraway had admired Father Martin from the moment he had seen Chalk Talk. However, he knew less about Mae. "Although we came from very similar backgrounds, both of us were from the South and both of us had been raised as Baptists with a deep distrust of Catholics," Jamie recalls,

> I didn't get to know Mae as quickly as I got to know Father Martin. He is very open and friendly; you feel as if you've got a friend for life after your first 20 minutes with him. Mae is a bit more reserved. I knew how intelligent and dedicated she was, both to Father Martin and to Ashley, but I didn't understand the depth of her commitment to alcoholics until one day, while I was visiting, and I saw her with one of the patients.
>
> This young fellow was in pretty sorry shape, and he was not benefiting from the treatment at Ashley. There are very few people who would have dealt with him as Mae did. She never hesitated; she was going to do everything possible to help him, no matter the cost.
>
> After Mae finally determined that the young man had some relatives in California who were willing to take care of him, she arranged for him to take a plane there. She would drive him to the airport, and one of his relatives would pick him up. But before he left, Mae had the nurses help

him get cleaned up, then she took him downtown shopping for new clothes. "I don't want him to be ashamed on the plane or when he sees his family," Mae explained.

When I asked her where the money was coming from for all of these expenses, Mae explained that she would take it from a special scholarship fund she and Father had started for just such emergencies, and if there wasn't enough money in the fund, and there usually wasn't, then she would just use her own money.

I went with Mae to the airport. She walked the man to the gate to make sure he got safely on the plane. She hugged him, very briefly, and then turned around quickly. At that moment, I saw that Mae was crying. I had never seen her cry before, and it was at that moment I realized there was no one too rich or too poor for Mae's love. She did not show emotion or affection as quickly as some people, but underneath her ladylike demeanor, Mae Abraham is one of the most gentle and caring people on earth.

Mae and Father told the story of their recovery as often as possible at Ashley, and Leonard remembers that Mae continued to function as she always had. "By this time, Mae had acquired quite a reputation in the field as one of the founders of Ashley," Leonard recalls.

She could have sat back and basked in her accomplishments, but she never did that. She still answered calls for help whenever she could, and that occurred frequently since she was known in the Aberdeen community for being available whenever there was a need.

Mae would often bring these people to Ashley if she felt they would benefit from residential treatment. She would have the staff check their health insurance and consult with the family, then see how Ashley could help. There were occasions, however, when there was no one to pay for the patient's treatment. Very soon after Ashley opened, Mae began to recognize the need for what she called a "scholarship fund" so that Ashley could help people who would otherwise not be able to get help. Once such a fund was established, some patients were given full scholarships.

How wise she was in this regard. As a result of Mae and Father's refusal to admit patients based only on their ability to pay, there was always a wonderful mix of people from all walks of life. In this way, our patients could better understand that addiction knows no social or class boundaries. We are in this together, bound by two things: our disease and our desire to get well.

As our reputation began to grow, prominent and well-known people started coming to Ashley for treatment, and they were accorded the same treatment as the student or the engineer or the plumber. On the outside, a patient may have been known as a successful athlete or entertainer, but at Ashley, he or she was simply a person with a disease who needed to get better.

Father Martin's presence was a source of comfort to the patients. Although he was almost 60 years old by the time Ashley opened, he was as dynamic as ever: brimming with good humor, health, and happiness. He was the personification of sobriety, and the patients sensed this. In fact, Father Martin imposed strict guidelines, not only on his own behavior, but also on the behavior of every staff member at Ashley. "We wanted our patients to see what sobriety is about, and they could best see that through our example," Father recalls.

I like to use the analogy of the duck: if you look like a duck, fly like a duck, sound like a duck, and

quack like a duck, you are probably a duck. Well,
I would tell the patients over and over and over
again, if you look like an alcoholic, smell like an
alcoholic, sound like an alcoholic, and think like
an alcoholic, you are probably an alcoholic. But if
you're truly sober, you will look like it, sound like
it, think like it, and act and react like it.

By this time, Father had made several more films about different facets of addiction and recovery, and as the patients viewed
these films over the course of their treatment, they began to iden-
tify more and more closely with the sober life. "Those films
inspired people," Leonard recalls. "I remember one woman saying to me, after seeing one of Father's films, 'he lifts people up.'
That is Father's primary contribution to Ashley, by his very existence, by his very nature, he lifts every one of us up, every day.
His presence and philosophy permeate every corner of Ashley."

In September of 1983, nine months after Ashley opened its
doors to its first five patients, a ribbon-cutting ceremony was
held, followed by a reception. Almost a thousand people attended: board members, donors, friends, family, former patients, grateful family members, and directors of other treatment centers.

Ashley still looked very much like a grand estate, with its mile-
long winding driveway lined with evergreens, its stone buildings,
and its lawns extending almost to the water's edge. The leaves on
the trees had begun to turn glorious shades of gold and red in the
cool autumn weather, and the sun glistened off the Chesapeake
Bay. Noble Hall was so impressive—with its oak floors, huge
windows with the view of the bay, beautiful furnishings, high
ceilings, and the exquisite center staircase that Mae had worked
so hard to preserve—that it could have been featured in
Architectural Digest.

In fact, so many people walked through the building commenting on its beauty that it did begin to seem as if Noble Hall
were being featured on a house tour. In some ways, it was. Given
the restoration and repairs that had been completed, a property

Noble Hall. (Courtesy of Father Martin.)

that had fallen into disrepair was once again one of the loveliest estates in Maryland.

At the beginning of the dedication ceremony, the Most Reverend Francis Murphy of the Archdiocese of Baltimore blessed Noble Hall, dedicating its work to the glory of God and the healing of the sick. Although Father Martin and Mae asked several of the dignitaries to say a few words, they did not want too much time taken up by official speeches or proclamations. They did want to be sure that Sam and Mary Jane Noble were recognized for their extraordinary generosity and faith in the project. However, Sam Noble "did not want to be singled out for special attention," Leonard Dahl recalls; "he said that just seeing Ashley thriving was all the reward he needed."

Mae remembers that during the official ribbon-cutting ceremony, Alex was standing off to the side holding her grandson, Tommy, who was two years old at the time. Suddenly, Tommy spotted his grandmother standing with Father Martin, Archbishop Murphy, and the others. Tommy began to cry for his grandmother and to reach out his arms for her to hold him.

Mae realized that she should have been concerned as Tommy's cries grew louder and louder, but instead, she felt nothing but gratitude and pleasure. "I looked toward my little grandson reaching out for me," Mae recalls,

> and I suddenly remembered what the last 20 years had been all about. Father Martin had enabled me

Sam and Mary Jane Noble at the dedication ceremony of Noble Hall in September of 1983. (Courtesy of Father Martin.)

to find sobriety, and because of him, I had been able to keep my family together. In gratitude for that, I had been determined to help Father Martin to recover, and to start Ashley so that his work could continue. At this magic moment we were celebrating the opening of Ashley, and my little grandson was calling out for me—what better symbol of the effects of sobriety—and what better reward could I have asked for?

As Ashley became more and more successful, people would ask Mae why she continued to remain in the background, shunning publicity and recognition. She explained that the only reward or recognition she needed she got every day from her family and from the patients at Ashley.

Father Martin couldn't avoid recognition, however. Even before Ashley had been established, his reputation as one of the most effective speakers in the field of alcoholism was secure. Now, with the added publicity of Ashley, demands for interviews increased. "Mae would disappear when the reporters arrived," Father recalls, "leaving me holding the bag." Invariably, the articles would praise Father's ability as a speaker. "Father Joseph C. Martin gave his famous Chalk Talk on Alcohol to a standing-room-only audience in Springfield last night," read an article from the *Springfield News,* published in Springfield, Pennsylvania, and it was typical of other articles that were written about Father. "The popular, dynamic speaker kept the assembled crowd captivated for over an hour with his flowing words, humorous anecdotes, bits of advice, and detailed descriptions of alcoholics' problems."

Another newspaper, *The Star,* published an account of Father's address to a crowd of one thousand people in Chicago, describing him as "the patron saint" in "the battle against alcoholism."

Often, he would be given the keys to a city or be declared an honorary citizen. In 1986 Loyola College, his alma mater, presented him with the Andrew White Medal, in recognition of his "contributions to the welfare of the people of Maryland." The ceremony took place in the chapel on Loyola's campus, and Father enjoyed the day, not only because of the honor that was bestowed upon him, but also because it provided an occasion for him to see many old friends. A few months later, Father was honored with the Father Kelly Award by Loyola High School, the high school he had attended 50 years earlier.

The *Professional Counselor,* a journal that is read by almost everyone in the field of alcoholism recovery, published an article in its Fall 1986 issue entitled "Father Martin Comes West." The journalist who wrote the story, Ed Hearn, provided his readers with a classic "tease" opening paragraph by mentioning Father's "love affair"; however, it was an affair, he quickly explained,

> between this jolly little priest and thousands of people in the alcohol/drug field. At the Marriott Hotel, they had hugged him in elevators, in the lobby, and in the coffee shop, thanking him for helping them through his films, writings, and teachings.

He was part celebrity, part guru, and always the priest. "Thank you. You're too kind. Gee, that's nice of you to think of me. Thank you. God bless you," he told a friendly woman who had given him some "warm fuzzies" [slippers] in the lobby. When a man introduced himself, Father Martin replied, "Joe, I hear you're doing great things up there in Tennessee. Keep up the good work."

The author then described meeting Father Martin again six months later:

This energetic phenomenon was on the road again, although he now limits his appearances to a couple a week. He had been in Hartford and Boise this week, and added the Everett, Washington, appearance because of its proximity to Boise and to help the Evergreen people [raise money] to buy some furniture for their non-profit recovery homes.

The airplane unloaded, and out walked the white-haired priest, a bounce in his step, turning to say good-bye to a flight attendant. He still had that marvelous twinkle in his eyes as we greeted one another and headed toward the baggage department, stopping along the way to change his return flight so he could be back in Maryland a day early.

At the ticket counter, he inquired of the clerk about his ancestry, which was Greek. [Father had visited Greece with the Navy in 1974.] Within minutes, he was calling the clerk by his first name and talking about Greece. Asked if he was always that friendly with people, he responded, "Do you know how many people in this world don't hear many friendly words? Most people gripe at clerks like him. I try to say their names twice, out loud, and then I can usually remember them. All of us

Father Martin signing his autograph for Nils Lofgren, one of his many admirers. (Courtesy of Mrs. Mae Abraham.)

want to be loved and cared about! I just want to do my little bit."

In 1988 Cardinal John J. O'Connor of New York used his weekly column, "From My Viewpoint," which appeared in the New York Archdiocesan weekly, to praise Father Martin's work. "Ashley is a beautiful spot on beautiful grounds," the Cardinal wrote,

> and that's nice, but not critical. What *is* critical to the program is Father Martin and his associates. I have known him for maybe 15 years. I don't know anyone, anywhere, more sensitive, more compassionate, or more knowledgeable about alcoholism. Graduates of Ashley come away singing his praises. Many of them couldn't sing at all before they met him; more than a few couldn't even talk rationally.

In 1992 Norman Vincent Peale, celebrating the fortieth anniversary of his best-seller, *The Power of Positive Thinking,* decided to honor three people "who have put the principles of positive thinking in their lives," and Peale asked members of his board to submit nominations. Christine Benati, who had remained close to Father and Mae even after she completed her term as a board member of Ashley, nominated Father, and he was named one of the honorees.

Father took most of this recognition in stride, never losing sight of the real purpose of his life. It was not as easy as Father made it appear, however. Conway Hunter frequently attended the major conferences at which Father spoke, and he would stand by as hundreds of people crowded around Father to speak with him, touch him, and ask for his autograph. "Father was the consummate performer," Hunter recalls,

> but it was actually exhausting and enervating for him. Because he was such a talented speaker, making it all look so easy and natural, people never suspected that after speaking for more than an hour, he would be tired and want nothing more than to be quiet, to have a simple meal with a couple of friends.
>
> Father would never express these needs; he always put others first, and he sincerely enjoyed meeting people. But over the course of our friendship, I came to realize that Father Martin is actually a shy man who loves simple things. We'd take him to really nice restaurants, and as often as not he'd order spaghetti. We'd be sitting with some important people, but he'd usually single out someone young at the table—the daughter or son of someone—and ask him or her about school, career, hobbies. He loves talking to waiters and waitresses.
>
> He had become a "public" figure; there was nothing he could do about it, even if he wanted to. But I will never forget a particularly "private" glimpse I once had of him—it really endeared him to me. After he gave a talk at my facility, he

came back to my home to spend the night before flying back to Maryland the next day. At about 1:00 in the morning, I heard noises downstairs, and at first I became alarmed. However, as I listened more closely, I realized that it was Father Martin going to the kitchen to have a midnight snack. It's a little thing, I know, but when you only see a man in public settings where people treat him as larger than life, you tend to forget the other side—the side that just wants to sit at a kitchen table at 1:00 in the morning and have a peanut butter and jelly sandwich and a glass of milk.

Terry Gorski, whose reputation in the field had been growing steadily from the time in the early 1970s when he first viewed Father's Chalk Talk, also remembers the way that Father's public life was often at odds with his spiritual and emotional needs.

I had spent a few days at Ashley doing some consulting work during the mid 1980s, and when it was time for me to go to the airport, we realized that Father had to be there at the same time to fly to a speaking engagement. Of course, I offered to drive him. Father and I had been in meetings with the staff at Ashley for several days—long sessions that left us tired at the end of the day. Now, he was going off to speak that evening.

He sat in the passenger seat as I drove, and as I looked over, I realized that Father was reading the Divine Office. I didn't disturb him of course, but I noticed his concentration, and I also noticed that his entire countenance had changed—he seemed secure and at peace.

When he finished, I asked him what he had been reading, and he explained that reading each day from his daily breviary was not only an obligation of his priesthood, it was essential to his spir-

itual health. "I am a priest," Father explained to
me. "I believe, more than I believe anything else
in this world, that my daily Mass and my daily
prayers to God are far more important than anything else I do. And I pray to God every day to
give me the strength I need to do my work. It is
in His hands. Do you know how many times I
have given the Chalk Talk? Well, this is my work.
This is what I do. It is a major part of my priestly vocation, so I pray to God to help me do it
right, day after day, so that I can—through Him—
help others."

It was at that time that I began to realize how
few people realize what this man's priesthood
means to him: so many of us see the Roman collar and call him Father, but we only see these
things as symbols—they are not symbols at all,
they are the very essence of his life. All of his
good work in alcoholism is a manifestation of his
priesthood. He would do these things with or
without the recognition—and sometimes I think
he would prefer to do it without quite so much
recognition.

By 1985 Father Martin had been a priest for 38 years, more
than half of his life, and he thanked God each morning for the
gift of his vocation. However, ever since he had been asked to
relinquish his membership in the Sulpician Society years before,
he had felt a void. "I still did my best to fulfill all of my duties as
a priest," Father recalls,

but I always felt a great sorrow that I could not
place those two letters after my name, S.S., for the
Society of Saint Sulpice. They meant so much to
me, ever since the time when I was a high-school
kid working on the switchboard at the seminary.
I just admired the Sulpicians so much that I wanted to be one of them from the beginning of my

studies. But I tried not to think about it. I just
considered it a cross that Jesus Christ intended for
me to bear, and I left it at that.

The Society was never far from Father's mind or heart, however. In fact, while he was on a trip to California in 1985 to speak
in Santa Cruz, Father asked the man who was driving him back
to the airport if he would mind making a detour to Mountain
View, so that Father could again see the seminary where he had
taught for seven years after his ordination. Father still remembers
the occasion.

> As I walked through the front entrance, the first
> person I saw was Father Gerry Brown. He had
> been a student of mine in the 1950s, and the year
> before, in 1985, he had been elected Provincial
> Superior of the Society. Gerry is one of the finest
> priests I have ever had the privilege of knowing,
> and I congratulated him.
>
> I asked him out of the blue if there were any
> possibility of returning to the Society. You can
> just imagine my astonishment when Father told
> me that at a recent meeting of the Provincial
> Council, they had decided they would invite me
> back. "We've been following your career," Gerry
> said, "and the work you are doing is very much in
> the spirit of the Society's mission. We are very
> proud of you." Then he asked me if I would
> "consider" returning to the Society. That's the
> word he used: "consider." Can you imagine being
> asked to consider something for which you had
> prayed for almost ten years? I was speechless.
>
> When I got back to Maryland, I contacted
> Archbishop Borders, under whom I was serving,
> and asked him if it would be all right if I returned
> to the Society. He said yes; as always, he was kind
> and gracious, and within a month, I was re-instat-

ed. I remember telling Mae that if I died the next day, I'd die happy.

In 1989 Father Martin was invited to Ireland to give several lectures and to appear on the "Gaye Byrne Show," a two-hour television program that aired each Saturday night. (This show was as popular in Ireland as the "Ed Sullivan Show" had been in the United States.) Byrne had seen Chalk Talk and wanted Father on the show. Father presented a slightly shorter version of his Chalk Talk, and the effect was extraordinary. The audience was mesmerized; even the host, known for responding to his guests with remarks intended to make the audience laugh, seemed awestruck. "Father, you are an invaluable source of knowledge," Byrne said at the end of the presentation, shaking his head in amazement. "The world needs to hear what you have to say."

The next day several people recognized Father at the airport, calling out "I seen you last night on the telly," thanking him for talking about alcoholism with such honesty and intelligence. "Come back to Ireland soon," one man called to Father, "we need you here."

Father Martin had become accustomed to his growing popularity—actually, he had no choice in the matter—but what pleased him most were the letters he received. Pat Hitchcock has saved hundreds of them; they are testimony to the impact Father was having on the lives of thousands of people. "Dear Father Martin," a typical letter reads,

> I just had to write and tell you how much you did for me on the Saturday evening you spoke here [in British Columbia]. I have been trying to get sober for 12 years, had 52 slips, been in hospitals 11 times and jails 12 times, stumbling and living in hell. I had been in treatment 3 weeks when you came. I was in a state of mental disorder such as I had never known before; the day you spoke was my fourth day of real hell; I thought I was going insane for sure. You were talking and I was trying to listen. Then, all of a sudden, Father, you

said about how to stay sober, you said the 12 steps were the answer, you shouted out do them and I came right out of my chair.

Father since then I have repeated this story at least 20 times. You got through to me as though someone turned a 500 watt light on in my head. It was and still is so clear how I also can stay sober, Father. I thought I was hopeless, completely hopeless, and now I know I am not. Thank you from the bottom of my heart. I shall never forget you and I know now that God must have directed me to you in order that I could be restored to sanity. I spoke to you briefly that evening, shook your hand, and thanked you. I am staying at the treatment center now, Father, doing the steps, and next Friday will take the Fifth Step, for the first time in my life, thanks to you.

Father often read the letters aloud to Mae and Leonard, but despite such gratification, he was still working too hard. No one was more aware of this than Mae. She realized that too many demands were being made on Father's energy and time: not only was he spending several hours a day at Ashley, he was also spending about a third of his time traveling around the country and the world to speaking engagements.

By this time, he was so well respected in the field that he was invited to deliver the keynote addresses at many conferences. On these occasions, Father would often stand for up to two hours, first giving his presentation and then answering questions from the audience. His legs would grow tired, and he complained to Mae about pain in his knees. Mae insisted that Father see a doctor who subsequently performed surgery on one knee and diagnosed a hairline fracture in the other. (As a result, Father delivered his talks sitting on a stool for a few weeks.) But in addition to the surgery, what Father really needed, the doctor said, was to take it easy.

As a result, Mae and Pat Hitchcock tried to space Father's commitments, and they arranged for an Ashley employee to accompany him on his trips to lessen the strain on him. Mae began to "encourage" Father to watch his diet (with limited success); his weight has always been a matter of concern. And when Father was home, she arranged his schedule in such a way that he could take a nap during the day. (Lou Bantle likes to tease Father about his propensity to take these naps during Ashley board meetings. Father responds that he spends the first half of board meetings trying to look intelligent "as if I know what's going on," and the last half "trying to stay awake.")

In 1989 Father's brother Leo died of pneumonia, and in 1992 his sister Marie died of cancer. Although Father's work in establishing Ashley had consumed much of his time, he had always remained in close contact with his brothers and sisters, and he had performed the christenings, and then the weddings, of many of his nieces and nephews. "I knew Marie and Leo were with God," Father recalls, "but we had been close as children, and proud of each other as adults. I miss them." In addition, within a period of two years, Mae lost three brothers, Roger, Junior, and Claude, and she too felt deep grief.

It took the loss of these family members to finally convince Father to slow down and take the time he needed to enjoy his family, his friends, and his home. And the activity that he began to enjoy most was being at home when Mae and Tommy's grandchildren, Tommy and Audrey, were there, particularly during the summer months when they could play in the pool. Tommy and Audrey, who were only a year apart in age, loved Father Martin, and they spent time playing with him, listening to his stories, and providing Father with what he describes as "pure childish fun." In addition, Father still remembers the "refreshing way" that the children responded to him, for example, when he began to wear hearing aids.

"When Audrey heard I had to wear hearing aids, she said to her grandmother, 'Poor Father.' But I told her I was glad to have

The last photograph taken of all the Martin children. Rear, left to right: Edward, Father Martin, Leo, Bernard. Front, left to right: Frances, Marie, Dorothy. (Courtesy of Father Martin.)

them, and she said, 'Well, that's good, you won't have to keep saying "Huh?" anymore.'"

However, Father also remembers the Sunday morning when Tommy, who was about five years old, was inattentive and disruptive at Mass. Afterward, at brunch, Tommy was still in a grumpy mood, and Father began to kid around and tell funny stories in an attempt to lighten his spirits. "Tommy folded his little arms," Father recalls, "gave me a grim look, and said, 'Father, I'm just in no mood for your silly jokes.'"

Father then turned his attention to four-year-old Audrey, who had always been a picky eater, and tried to entice her to eat healthy foods. "What healthy foods do you eat?" Audrey asked Father. After naming the ones that he thought she would like, Audrey interrupted and asked, "If you eat those foods, why do you have such a big belly?" In true W.C. Fields' fashion, Father replied, "Audrey, how would you like a kick in the teeth?"

Father Martin getting a new hairdo from Tommy and Audrey at the Abrahams' backyard pool. (Courtesy of Mrs. Mae Abraham.)

"What's that?" Audrey asked.

"Just keep it up and you'll find out," Father replied.

Tommy and Audrey brought great pleasure to their grandparents as well. The children visited Mae, Tommy, and Father every other weekend, and quite often in between. Father recalls that he had never seen Mae and Tommy so happy.

> They loved being grandparents. For a time, the house had grown quiet—after all, it was just Mae, Tommy, and me shuffling around, and for so many years, we were utterly consumed with getting Ashley going. Then suddenly we had these two happy, active youngsters around us all the time, and we had the pleasure of watching them grow.

Mae was dedicated to her grandchildren, of course, but she remained equally dedicated to Tommy and Father. People who came into contact with Mae recognized almost immediately her kindness and her generosity, and they respected her intelligence and determination—she had been the driving force behind getting Ashley built and everyone knew it.

Mae and Father's unusual relationship has, on several occasions, led to (very humorous) confusion. Shortly after Ashley opened, for example, Father, Mae, and Leonard instituted the practice of holding a weekly graduation ceremony for those patients who would be completing their treatment during that week. It was (and still is) a wonderful opportunity for all the patients to hear the graduates describe their experiences at Ashley and their hopes for the future. Family members are urged to attend this ceremony, and they too are invited to speak to the audience. Many are moved to tears by the honest and poignant remarks that the graduates make as a result of the transforming experience they have had at Ashley. It is also traditional for Father, Leonard, and Mae to say a few words of encouragement before the patients leave Ashley to re-enter the world.

On one such morning, a young patient was trying to express his gratitude for his newly found sobriety. He began by explaining how nervous he was and how he did not want to speak for very long, but he felt obligated to express his thanks to the people who had saved his life. "I just want to thank God for my recovery," he said haltingly. "I want to thank God for helping Father and Mae start Ashley, and I want to thank Father Martin and Mae for having Leonard." The audience exploded into laughter.

Although Mae, Father, and Tommy would never have to work as hard as they did during the years of fund-raising and in the early days of operation, Ashley still consumed much of their time and energy. Leonard's appointment as executive director had relieved them of the enormous burden of worrying about many of the day-to-day responsibilities. However, not long after Ashley opened, Mae and Father realized they would soon run out of room.

As a result, they spent the next two years refurbishing the carriage house in order to provide space for offices, meeting rooms, and living quarters. It was far easier to raise the money needed for this project than it had been to restore Noble Hall. There was less work to be done, and since Ashley was operating so successfully, potential donors could see how their money would be used. In addition, Ashley had a generous and loyal friend in Lou Bantle. Soon after he had joined Ashley's board, he had arranged for UST, a highly successful Fortune 500 company, to provide matching funds for all donations made to Ashley at the annual fund-raisers. In addition, Lou interested many of his colleagues in the project. Ralph Rossi, a UST Vice President and one of Lou's best friends, became a member of the board of directors of Ashley, and he also became a generous benefactor.

Lou also began to send employees to Ashley for treatment through UST's Employee Assistance Program. Jim Cassidy, who had recovered at Ashley shortly after it opened, was not only a UST employee, but also one of Lou Bantle's closest friends, and his recovery, Lou recalls, "helped me to see, close up, the value of Ashley's program and methods. I cared very much for Jim and his family. To have him come back to work and to his family with his health and spirit restored symbolized the work Father and Mae were doing for other people just like Jim."

Jim recalls the extraordinary respect he developed for Mae and Father during his stay at Ashley.

> When Lou suggested that I go to Ashley, I was scared. I decided that I would make a good first impression, so I got all dressed up in my best three-piece suit. I don't know why, maybe I thought that would help me to somehow maintain control, or that people wouldn't think I had all that much of a problem if I were well dressed. As a matter of fact, when I first arrived, one of the nurses actually thought I was there to apply for a job as a counselor.
>
> Not only was I scared and angry, I was also in denial. However, Father greeted me with such warmth and good humor that I began to relax and feel better about being there. Ironically, dur-

212

ing one of his talks to the patients, he mentioned
how scared he had been when he entered Guest
House and how comforting it was for him when
Austin Ripley greeted him with great sincerity
and warmth. I felt like saying, "Father, do you
realize that's exactly what you did for me?"

I don't remember precisely when I met Mae; I
just remember that it seemed as if she was always
nearby, checking on things, talking to patients,
making sure we were comfortable. You just kind
of felt that you would be okay because Mae was
looking after you.

But Ashley is no resort. The treatment was intense, and there were many times when I just did-
n't want to come to terms with my addiction, but
I had no choice. I remember telling Father that by
the end of my treatment, I had learned enough
about alcoholism and addiction that I would
never be able to enjoy drinking again. "Well, I'm
happy to hear that," Father said with a big smile.
"Glad we spoiled your drinking for you."

Several years later, after Jim had become a member of the
board of directors, he arrived at Ashley wearing casual clothes.
"That time," he recalls, "I looked so disheveled that one of the
nurses thought I was there for treatment."

One of the patients admitted to Ashley at about this time was
Dr. Adam van Savage, the psychiatrist who had treated Mae during the first year of her sobriety. Dr. Van (as Mae called him) had
become a good friend, often visiting the Abraham home, where
he loved to play gin rummy with Tommy or go water skiing with
Alex. Mae recalls the way she "tried to repay" Dr. van Savage:

He was so helpful to other alcoholics, but he was
unable to sustain his own sobriety. He suffered for
many years from cancer, and toward the end of his
illness, he needed much care and attention. Father
and Micki counseled him, and I did everything I

could to make him comfortable, wrapping him in hot blankets at night.

When he was too ill to remain at Ashley, we brought him to the hospital, where Leonard, Micki, Father, and I took turns visiting him. He told us that because of Ashley he was able to live his last days free of addiction.

During his last days of life, rather than go back on drugs, he opted to have his spinal cord severed. It was astounding to see the lengths Dr. Van would go to die free from drugs. It was an example for all who think working the program is too hard. We've had thousands of patients at Ashley, but I will never forget him.

The Carriage House was entirely restored and ready for use in 1985, and Mae and Father decided to name the lecture room Carpenter Hall, in gratitude to their friend, Russ Carpenter, who had bequeathed Ashley $75,000—money that had been so desperately needed during the final period of restoration of Noble Hall. With the Carriage House restored, Ashley had the capacity to serve 45 patients, but as the census grew, there were times it was obvious that even more space was needed. At about this time, Mae remembers standing with Lou Bantle looking at the 15 acres of land to the left of Noble Hall. "That would be a perfect spot for a new building to take care of our needs," Lou noted.

Mae couldn't have agreed more. Ashley had been even more successful than she and Father had ever hoped, and more and more people, especially former patients, were referring patients to Ashley. Mae realized that in order for Ashley to serve their needs, another building would be needed. Mae spoke of this at several board meetings, leading Sam Noble to joke that he believed she was suffering from a severe case of "buildingitis," but in fact Mae was right. She was beginning to realize that Lou Bantle would probably be a primary source of support for the project, in gratitude for his own sobriety, but also as a reflection of his extraordinary foresight.

Long before there would be a Bantle Hall, however, Mae, Tommy, Leonard, and Father were determined to build a chapel. This would provide a place for Father to offer Mass for the community and for Leonard to hold a weekly ecumenical worship service. It would be a house of God to which all were invited daily to share God's peace. Father insisted that the chapel be non-denominational, so that "each patient, no matter what his or her beliefs, could worship freely. It makes no sense not to have a chapel in a place where the soul, even more than the body, needs healing."

Mae and Father arranged for a fund-raiser to be held to cover the cost of building the chapel, and on the very first day, more than $60,000 was raised—all of which would be matched by UST. (Together, Mae, Father, and Tommy pledged $20,000.) The cost of the chapel was $250,000, but Pat Hitchcock recalls that it was a little easier to raise funds. "All Mae had to do was ask, and many were willing to give. Mae and Father had proven, beyond a doubt, the worth of Ashley, and there were those who considered it an honor to contribute."

The chapel, completed in December of 1985, is an extension of nature—through the huge stained-glass panel behind the altar one can watch (and feel the warmth of) the sun as it rises. The panel, flanked on each side by panes of clear glass, composes the entire back wall of the chapel, providing an unobstructed view of the Chesapeake Bay. The motif in the stained glass depicts Ashley's crest, a wreath of eight oak leaves ranging in color from lightest green to burnt amber—a symbol of nature's eternal cycle of healing and regeneration.

The wreath was conceived by Father Martin and drawn by Cathy Peluso, who happens to be Mae's niece and Micki Thomas's daughter. No artist could have better understood the cycle of life that existed at Ashley: a year after her own recovery, Cathy had seen her own mother return to a happy and productive life.

Despite the extraordinary beauty of every aspect of Ashley— from the stately buildings to the acres of perfectly manicured

The Chapel at Father Martin's Ashley. (Courtesy of Mrs. Mae Abraham.)

lawns and the view of the Chesapeake Bay—the majority of patients and visitors are still most deeply affected by the sight of the stained-glass window. "If you ask me what I think when I hear the word Ashley," a former patient wrote to Father, "it is that magnificent window reflecting color and warmth and hope onto the faces of the patients sitting in the Chapel. That wreath encircles all of us in a ring of hope, long after we leave."

Around the door of the Chapel are three panels of stained glass, one above and one on either side (donated by good friends of Ashley, Ralph Rossi and Jack Africk). Depicted in these panels, in addition to the Holy Family, are symbols of many of the world's religions, a Star of David, for example, and a shamrock. However, the artist who designed the panels, W.O. Miles, was well aware of the role that humor plays in recovery and of Father Martin's reputation as one of the best storytellers around. He remembered in particular one joke—one of Father's favorites—that seemed to help the patients realize that although the disease of alcoholism is deadly serious, recovering alcoholics don't have to be.

Father would ask the patients if they had heard about the drunk walking down the street with a penguin. A police officer spotted them and told the drunk to take the penguin to the zoo. The next day, the same police officer again saw the same drunk walking down the street with the penguin. "I thought I told you to take him to the zoo," the police officer yelled. "I did, officer," the drunk replied. "He loved it. Today we're going to the library."

Without telling anyone at Ashley, Miles completed the stained-glass panels containing the symbols of the religions of the world, but in the bottom right hand corner, he also inserted a one-inch-square piece of glass containing the figure of a penguin. It is Father's favorite symbol. "Long after I've been fertilizing dandelions, people will look at it and wonder what religion it's a symbol of," he notes, "and I'll get a chuckle in the great beyond."

The Chapel was completed by Christmas Eve, 1985, and Father offered Midnight Mass for the first time at Ashley. More than one hundred patients and friends attended, and the music in the Chapel on that evening reminded Father of the beautiful music that he had so loved as a seminarian. (The organ had also been donated by Ralph Rossi and his family.)

Shortly after the chapel was completed, Father, Mae, and Tommy had a plaque prepared and placed on the outside of the building, directly under one of the stained-glass panels, that reads:

> Chapel of the Holy Family
> dedicated in memory of
> James and Marie Martin
> Arthur and Molly Ashley
> Alex and Anna Abraham.

"The Chapel completed Ashley for Father," Leonard Dahl has observed.

> We had everything we needed for our patients' physical needs until then, but Father felt strongly that there was now a place where their spiritual needs could be met as well. I believe that if you ask Father where in the world he is most content, he would respond, "the Chapel."

CHAPTER EIGHT

Good Things Will Happen
in Your Life

B y 1986 several changes were occurring in the field of alcohol treatment that were having an enormous impact on facilities such as Ashley. Health insurance companies were beginning to limit the amount of coverage they would provide for long-term stays in residential facilities, and, as a result, many of the treatment centers that had opened during the early 1980s, a period of enormous growth in the field, were now beginning to close. In fact, by 1992, forty percent of the alcohol and drug addiction treatment centers in the United States had gone out of business.

Despite these trends, Ashley was not only surviving, it was flourishing. It was ranked among the top five facilities in the country, and more and more people were being referred to Ashley. Most experts would have advised Mae and Father Martin to continue to do precisely what they were doing, and from a business standpoint, they would have been right.

However, Micki Thomas, who had been placed in charge of developing and directing the treatment programs at Ashley and who had continued to take courses and seminars in order to remain informed of new developments in the field, was becoming more and more aware of the problem of relapse among alcoholics and drug addicts. Micki had also become aware of the work that Terry Gorski had been doing for some years in the area of relapse therapy.

Furthermore, Micki knew first-hand the agony of relapse, for she herself had suffered several relapses—in fact she had almost died—before she was finally able to achieve a lasting sobriety. She was aware of the resistance to Gorski's work because it was new, and she was aware that professionals in the field felt constricted by the new financial climate: at a time when nearly half of the treatment facilities in the country were closing, who would dare to invest resources in an untried, unproven relapse-prevention program? However, because of her own relapse history, Micki felt that Gorski's program was custom fitted for all relapsers.

Micki traveled to Chicago to be trained by Gorski and to learn first-hand about his relapse program; in fact, she was the first relapse counselor to be certified by him. When Micki returned to Ashley, she persuaded Father Martin, Mae, and Leonard to have Terry integrate a relapse program into Ashley's curriculum. No one knew better than Father of the need for such a program: "I had often said in my conversations and in my lectures," Father recalls,

> that the disease of alcoholism "brooks of relapse."
> I loved the sound of that phrase, but I also knew
> the pain and suffering that relapse causes. I real-
> ized that Micki was right: our mission was to help
> addicted people to recover, and if the first round
> of treatment wasn't successful, then to simply
> bring relapsers back to undergo the very same
> primary treatment didn't make any sense to me.

Terry Gorski remembers the many visits he made to Ashley in order to help institute the relapse program; these visits enabled him to realize the depth and profundity of Father Martin's understanding of the disease.

> By the mid 1980s, people recognized Father as
> one of the leading spokespersons for the efficacy
> of the Twelve Steps, and of course they recog-
> nized him and Mae as the co-founders of one of
> the—if not the—best treatment facilities in the

world. What I began to realize as I sat for hours with Father and the rest of his staff was his deep understanding and love for the alcoholic.

Before I even traveled to Ashley to help implement the program, I spent five days at home watching every video that Father Martin had made, in the order in which he had made them. I remember saying to myself, "This is going to get boring and repetitive because after the first few tapes, I'll just be hearing the same stuff repeated over and over." But I was so wrong. By viewing those tapes, I was watching, in effect, the development of his knowledge, understanding, and compassion for the alcoholic, but there was more to it than that.

Father was fond of saying that Chalk Talk and his other talks were nothing more than a distillation of everything he had learned from Rip and Doc Green, and maybe he truly believed that, but those videotapes are all the evidence anyone will ever need to prove that Father Joseph Martin has developed, as a result of his lifelong dedication, a knowledge base and an understanding of the disease that few possess.

Furthermore, by this time, friends and family had begun to tease Father about his need to take short naps and about his short attention span. Well, he didn't exhibit those traits in our meetings. He listened quietly, to be sure, but then when it was time for someone to summarize or to ask good questions, it became apparent that Father Martin was the only one in the room who understood everything that had been said—he synthesized in such a way that suddenly everything became clear and logical. Because of him, we were able to put a program together in less than a month—a remarkably short time.

After the initial planning and implementation phase was complete, Terry returned to Ashley about four times a year for the next three years to oversee its development. Micki Thomas was placed in charge of the relapse program, and it was such a success that other residential treatment facilities began to recommend Ashley's program to their own patients who suffered relapse.

By this time, the need for more space at Ashley was greater than ever. The doctor's office and nurses' station were crowded together on the lower level of Noble Hall. Patients, staff, and visiting family members had to be fed in shifts in the two tiny dining rooms. These rooms were connected to the small kitchen by a narrow staircase, and the food-service staff had to trudge up and down the steps. Mae, Leonard, and Father shared one office, and the counselors' offices, Father remembers, "were wherever we could put them"; several were located in rooms under the Chapel. Living quarters were crowded: sometimes there were three patients assigned to a room suited for two. The laundry was located in the basement of the Carriage House, near the medical-records office.

With another building, the administrative, financial, and medical offices could be located in one place, along with a kitchen and dining room that could accommodate Ashley's growing population. In that way, Noble Hall and the Carriage House could be used exclusively as residential buildings.

There were no buildings left on the property to restore, however: this time around, a building would have to be designed and built—at a cost of about six million dollars. Mae, Tommy, and Father braced themselves for another round of fund-raising, anticipating a repeat of the "Seven Years of Begging" that had preceded the opening of Ashley. In 1988, to start the campaign off, Father, Tommy, and Mae together pledged $25,000 to be paid over five years. "We believed that we had no right to ask others to give," Father Martin recalls, "unless we had given first."

Mae had always known that she could count on the support of Lou Bantle, but she and Father were ebullient when Lou informed them that his company, UST, would pledge three mil-

222

lion dollars. (UST has been equally generous to scores of other charitable organizations, donating millions of dollars to the Miami Project, for example, to sponsor research for paralysis victims.) As a result of UST's magnanimous gift, construction could begin immediately. In addition to UST's donation, Lou and his wife Gini were also, Father recalls, "two of Ashley's most generous friends."

In 1989, shortly before construction began on the new building, Pat, Father, Micki, Tommy, and Leonard decided to honor Mae on the occasion of her twenty-fifth anniversary of sobriety with a surprise dinner. The planning took months, and they succeeded in preventing Mae from discovering their secret, but it wasn't easy. During the celebration, Pat stood at the podium and described just how difficult it had been. Pat's description is an indication of the way that Mae oversaw everything that went on at Ashley; nothing went unnoticed.

> In all my 15 years working with Father, Mae, and Tommy, this has been the most difficult task I've ever had. Believe me, Mae would make a wonderful private detective. If there is anything to be found, she will find it. At one point the printer called, and Mae knew it was he on the phone. Of course, she didn't know he was printing the program for the dinner and I couldn't talk about it with Mae in the room, so I told him that I didn't think we would be doing that project right now, hoping that he would realize I meant that we couldn't talk about it at the moment. But he didn't understand, and the poor man nearly had a heart attack. "What do you mean you're not going to do it?" he yelled. "I've got the paper ordered, I've got the color separation." I just said in my calmest voice, "I'll get back to you on that. Thank you very much."
>
> We soon realized that we simply couldn't make any of the plans at Ashley, so we started meeting

Alex Abraham with his children, Audrey and Tommy. (Courtesy of Mrs. Mae Abraham.)

in parking lots, at McDonald's, and at a local restaurant in Havre de Grace. During one of those meetings, we saw one of the employees from Ashley who had called in sick that day, and she saw us. Leonard just smiled and said, "We won't tell if you won't."

Pat then described the effect of Mae's sobriety on the entire Abraham family, explaining that because she was the only one of 11 children who was not an alcoholic, she had been filled with fear and anger before Mae helped her understand the disease of alcoholism. Pat also explained that she thought her sister Mae had lost her mind when she began working with a Catholic priest. "As a Baptist," Pat explained, "this just didn't make any sense to me. But through Mae, I came to know Father Martin, to respect him, and finally to love him."

Micki also paid tribute to Mae, telling everyone that Mae had saved her life, long after most people had given up on her. Alex spoke, as did Father and Leonard, followed by Father's sister Marie. Each speaker told a story about Mae, but each story had the same theme—Mae would go to any length to help others.

It was a wonderful celebration, held in Halas Hall, a large room located below the Chapel. The board members and their spouses attended, along with Archbishop Borders and Father Gerry Brown. Father Martin presented Mae with a piece of Steuben glass entitled "Excalibur"—a sterling sword with a gold handle embedded in the glass. Father explained that the silver symbolized the silver jubilee of Mae's sobriety, while the gold on the handle "symbolized the double quality of her years of sobriety."

Jamie Carraway got the warmest reception from the audience when he described an incident that had occurred at a recent Ashley graduation. The father of one of the patients asked his son to explain the roles of Father Martin, Mae, and Leonard. The patient explained: "Well you see, Father Martin stirs the waters up; Leonard calms them down. But everybody around here knows that it was Mae who built the pool for them to play in." That's probably as accurate a description as any to explain the way that these three people, with such diverse backgrounds, manage to work together day after day, year after year, helping others.

By 1990, as a result of the availability of funds, construction on the new building was proceeding quickly. It would take only a little more than a year for it to be completed. "UST gave much of the money," Lou Bantle recalls,

> but it was Mae who made it all happen. By this time, she had overseen the renovation of two buildings on the property and the construction of the Chapel; if she had ever decided to resign from Ashley, she could have had a highly successful career as a general contractor. Mae talked about wiring, plumbing, and air-conditioning systems like a pro. Nothing got by her. It was almost funny. Here's this lovely woman with a soft southern accent talking about work orders, shipments, construction schedules, and water tables as if she had been doing this all her life. We all watched her in awe.

Actually, Mae had the help of a well-known architect, Jerry Baxter, who had been put in charge of the project. He and Tommy discussed every aspect of the building—from locating a quarry in Port Deposit, Maryland, less than ten miles from Ashley, that could supply the same type of stone that had been used on the original buildings—to the placement of every light switch. Mae was still the perfectionist, believing as always that Ashley's patients deserved the best.

Father Martin remembers the year of construction, 1990, as different from the years working on the other buildings.

> Those early years were years of frustration and worry while we scrounged for money to continue. And we were always wondering if we would ever get done.
>
> But with the new building, Mae and I would just look at each other and marvel. As Mae would say, "It's a lot easier with money in the bank." We thanked God so often for Lou and Gini Bantle's generosity that it's a wonder they didn't float to heaven on the day the building was completed.

The task of furnishing and decorating the new building was left up to Mae, and after she consulted with an interior decorator, it became apparent that it could cost as much as one million dollars to furnish the enormous new structure. As a result, Gini Bantle suggested to Mae that they do it themselves, traveling to North Carolina where most of the major furniture companies had their factories and showrooms. Leonard traveled with Gini and Mae "to help out," but he quickly realized,

> There could not have been two other women in the world who needed a man's help less. Mae and Gini were indomitable—they went for hours on end without getting tired. We visited most of the showrooms, and for the life of me, I couldn't understand how they could keep all of the styles and colors straight. They were buying couches,

226

chairs, tables, beds, by the dozen, yet they remembered precisely which fabric they had chosen for which room. They lost me before we even finished choosing the lamps—I was of absolutely no use to them.

Gini wasn't satisfied with the price she was being quoted for the carpets, so she called the president of the carpet company, explained her mission, and got the price reduced.

That may very well have been one of the largest shopping sprees ever to occur in North Carolina, but when it was all over, Mae and Gini had managed to furnish the entire building for less than half of what the interior decorator had first claimed it would cost, and they had done it in less than a week.

Then, when the furniture started arriving at Ashley, I was even more amazed: Mae and Gini remembered where each piece belonged. By the time they were finished, that building was so beautifully appointed that people literally gasped when they walked in. Many people still talk about the decorating of the new building with a little bit of awe in their voices.

Soon after the new building was completed, Father made a motion at one of the board meetings to name it in honor of Lou Bantle, but Lou protested. "Look, Father," Lou said,

I didn't help so that I could get honor and glory, I helped so that alcoholics could benefit. Furthermore, I don't think it's a good idea for another reason. When UST bought a vineyard in Washington State in 1980, the board decided to name one of the main streets running through the vineyard after me—Bantle Boulevard. Well, less than a week after they got the signpost up with my name on it, Washington State had the worst freeze in more than 100 years. The entire crop was destroyed. My name would bring bad luck.

Father wasn't convinced, knowing that Lou Bantle had brought nothing but good luck—and generous donations—to Ashley. In what Father remembers as "the most assertive behavior I ever exhibited at one of the board meetings, I just looked at Lou and said, 'I'm chairman here, and it will be called Bantle Hall.'"

Although the new building was in use by the end of 1991, the dedication of Bantle Hall did not take place until May 31, 1992, and just as Father and Mae had done for the blessing of Noble Hall, they invited Ashley's many friends and supporters to join in the celebration. Father, Mae, and Tommy assisted as Gini and Lou Bantle fit the cornerstone in place and cut the ribbon, and Archbishop William H. Keeler of Baltimore (now his Eminence William Cardinal Keeler) blessed and dedicated the building.

Betty Ford was the keynote speaker, and as her husband, President Gerald Ford, listened, she opened her remarks with the traditional A.A. greeting: "Hi, my name is Betty and I'm an alcoholic." The Gatlin Brothers, old and loyal friends of Ashley, provided the entertainment, and Father then invited the more than 1,500 guests to enjoy an outdoor lunch.

Father Martin was so overcome with emotion that he found it difficult to speak to the assembled guests. He regained enough control after a few moments to tell a few jokes. But then he grew serious: "I have always said that if I could have a hand in making Ashley a reflection of Guest House, I would be happy," Father said.

> Well I am more than happy. I have had a small hand in creating a place that—and I never thought I would say this—is certainly on a par with Guest House. And it is primarily because of the generosity of UST, and especially of Gini and Lou Bantle. For the better part of our lives, Mae and I have talked about Ashley, begged for Ashley, labored for Ashley—now, with the help of so

228

Bantle Hall. (Courtesy of Mrs. Mae Abraham.)

> many kind and generous people, we no longer
> have to talk and labor and beg—we have been
> blessed, Ashley has been blessed, and words fall
> short in trying to express our gratitude to you.
>
> People who know the true value of money use
> it to help others, and Ashley is fortunate to have
> such people as friends. I have become tongue-tied
> in the face of your generosity, but fortunately for
> me, words are not necessary when communicat-
> ing with true friends.

With the opening of Bantle Hall, Ashley was able to accommodate 80 patients, and it continued to attract recognition and
praise, often from very famous people, including Nancy Reagan,
who had arranged, through her foundation, to provide money for
Ashley to institute an adolescent center. "State requirements pre-
vented that from happening," Father recalls, "but her visit was a
memorable one. She was moved to tears as she stood in the
Chapel overlooking the Bay, and again when she read aloud the
description of the leaves in the wreath and what they symbolized
to the people assembled."

Mae Abraham greets President Gerald Ford, along with Gini and Lou Bantle and Father Martin, at the dedication of Bantle Hall. (Courtesy of Mrs. Mae Abraham.)

President Ford and Mrs. Betty Ford with Reverend Gerald Brown (left) and his Eminence William Cardinal Keeler. (Courtesy of Father Martin.)

Father Martin greets Mrs. Betty Ford at the dedication of Bantle Hall. (Courtesy of Mrs. Mae Abraham.)

Jamie Carraway remembers the effect—or lack thereof—that interaction with such famous and successful people had on Mae.

> I remember spending a few days at Ashley, and every once in a while Mae would be called to the phone. At least three of those phone calls were from some of the most prominent people in the country at the time: one was a politician, one was the wife of a politician, and one was an entertainer.
>
> After a while, I began to realize that these very famous people were calling Mae just to say hello, just to hear her words of support and encouragement. I remember thinking that we should nickname Mae "the den mother of the rich and famous." But Mae never even mentioned those phone calls; they were just part of her work. She spent the same amount of time, and showed the same amount of concern, to anyone who called her.

Although the staff of Ashley scrupulously protects the privacy of all of its patients, some of the people who have recovered at Ashley have *chosen* to talk about their experiences. Michael Deaver, a close friend of Nancy and Ronald Reagan who served in the White House as one of the most influential members of Reagan's staff, is one of those patients. In 1987 he wrote a book entitled *Behind the Scenes,* and along with extraordinary descriptions of the Reagan presidency, he described his struggle with alcoholism, his fear that his alcoholism would have a negative effect on the Reagan presidency, and his recovery at Ashley.

> For many of the 28 days I underwent treatment at Ashley, I was paranoid, sure that every new patient was an undercover reporter for *The New York Times.* It was three weeks before I could stand up in an auditorium, identify myself, and tell my story. That was a turning point for me.

Left to right: Lou Bantle, Mrs. Betty Ford, President Gerald Ford, Gini Bantle, Rod Chandler, Father Martin, the Gatlin Brothers, and fans. (Courtesy of Mrs. Mae Abraham.)

At Ashley, I found people who had been in situations similar to mine. The disease had no prejudices. It is a great equalizer, whether you are in the public eye or not. The fears and emotional problems are pretty much the same. I met people who became sources of strength to me, some who had been in government and others who were simply trying to cope with life in a private way.

Father Martin won my everlasting respect with his patience, his gentle concern. There are more delicate ways of saying this, but the way I felt then was lower than squid shit.... Yet Father Martin never failed during the day to seek me out and tell me how much I was loved. You might be surprised how badly a grown person needs to hear that, even one who thinks he has acquired a layer of cynicism. I considered myself a religious per-

Audrey Abraham presents flowers to Nancy Reagan as Father Martin looks on. (Courtesy of Mrs. Mae Abraham.)

son, who had once planned on entering the ministry. But Father Martin brought me to the first real understanding of my God, just by talking with me. I went to Mass every morning I was there, and the service took on a new meaning for me. Praying with other alcoholics and an alcoholic priest, gave me a sense of God's love I have never known.

Mae felt that Ashley was "complete" with the opening of Bantle Hall, but as always, she worried about what would happen to Ashley when Father was "no longer there." Father, Tommy, and Alex would just groan when Mae began to talk about such things, until finally one day Alex declared that he had the perfect

Left to right: Mae Abraham, Mike Deaver, Nancy Reagan, and Father Martin at Ashley. (Courtesy of Mrs. Mae Abraham.)

solution, explaining that they could do the same thing with Father as Roy Rogers had done with his beloved horse, Trigger. Alex explained:

> We can have a good taxidermist stuff Father Martin; then we can place a small cassette recorder in his back. When the time comes for him to give a talk, we can prop him up at the podium and stick a cassette in the recorder. If we can get the taxidermist to find a way to get his mouth to move while the tape is playing, we can keep Father going well into the next century.

To this day, whenever people worry about Father Martin's health, Mae, Tommy, Alex, or Father tells them not to worry: they've already "made the necessary arrangements."

In a way, this is true. In fact, Ashley had been conceived because Mae wondered that night on the plane how Father's work could continue after his death. Mae and Father are no longer young; every decision they make is made with Ashley's future in mind. "We have enormous confidence in our board of directors," Father recalls. "We have some of the top businessmen and women in the country on that board, and we know that they will help us to secure Ashley's future, not only financially, but by ensuring that the people we hire and the decisions we make will provide the highest quality of treatment."

In 1992 Sam Noble, one of Ashley's best friends, was diagnosed with prostate cancer. Grateful that he would at least have time to put his affairs in order, he asked his wife, Mary Jane, to write letters of resignation to the many boards he had served on—all but Ashley. Instead, he decided to remain on the board for as long as he lived. "I love that place," he told Mary Jane, "and I love Father and Mae. Please don't ever lose contact with them." Father and Mae were devastated by the news, and they were even more devastated when Sam Noble was unable to attend the next board meeting—it was the first meeting he had missed in almost 13 years.

Sam Noble died on September 21, 1992, and Mary Jane Noble, his wife of 46 years, recalls the relationship he and Father had. "Bud loved Father Martin," she recalls.

> He loved his humility and his wisdom. He loved the fact that what he was doing with his life he was doing for others; there was no seeking of personal gain or personal recognition. That's why Bud stayed on the board until his death. He knew that Mae and Father had other very competent people on the board, but I believe he genuinely loved Ashley and Mae and Father. He loved going there every three months. Of all of the things that Bud helped create, I think he was most proud of and pleased with Ashley.
>
> We often talked about Mae and Father, how special they were, how unusual, how no one else in the world could have done what they did— most of us would never have been crazy enough

to even try in the first place. Bud would say that if there were ever a place where the hand of God was evident, it was Ashley, and one of the greatest pleasures of his life had been to be involved in such a place.

I remember that Father asked me if he could come to Oklahoma to visit Bud before he died, but Bud was in pain, and he did not want Father to see him ill. He asked me to thank Father for offering and to make sure that Father delivered the eulogy at his funeral. "I don't want him to make but one trip out here," Bud told me.

Father remembers Sam Noble's request as "one of the greatest honors I've ever had. Everyone knew Sam Noble as an oil magnate; I knew him as a dear friend." In fact, Father Martin and Mae had known Sam Noble for more than 15 years, and Tommy remembers how devastated they all were by his death.

Sam had been part of Ashley almost from the very beginning. Mae and Father had spoken with him at least once a week, every week, for 15 years. Furthermore, they saw him every three months at the board meetings. We never made a major decision without talking to Sam about it. He was our only "business head" for a very long time, but his heart was in Ashley as well.

Father had many friends, but I think he considered Sam Noble one of his best and closest friends, and I think Sam felt the same way about him. There was a terrible void, an emptiness, after his death, and it is still there. Shortly after Sam's death, Mae asked Mary Jane to take her husband's place on the board. Mary Jane accepted immediately, and this has given us great comfort.

Mae continued to do her best to keep Father Martin's schedule light enough to ensure that he get enough rest between trips, but it was almost impossible to say no to many of the requests that came in for him to speak. Furthermore, during the early 1990s, Lou Bantle had become one of the founders of an organization called the International Institute on Alcohol Education and Training, and Father made four trips to Russia under the auspices of the Institute. One of the Institute's goals was to bring Russian professionals to the United States for training in alcoholism treatment; another goal was to bring Russians to Ashley for treatment.

Within months the project had grown to such a degree that Lou's team was arranging for 100 Americans with training in alcoholism recovery and treatment—including Father Martin, of course—to travel to Russia to meet with their Russian counterparts. However, as everyone knew, in Russia there was no alcoholism treatment comparable to that in the United States. For the most part, alcoholics were placed in jails or in poorly equipped hospitals to dry out until they were able to return to work, only to have the cycle begin all over again.

Lou Bantle still remembers that during the second trip Father Martin spoke at an open meeting in the Palace of Youth, and the huge hall was packed. "Father had the same effect on that audience as he'd had on the thousands and thousands of people he had spoken to in the United States and in other countries," Lou Bantle recalls.

> Word of Father's arrival had spread, and the hall was filled to capacity. Furthermore, there were news crews everywhere, waiting to interview him. Fortunately, Jim Cassidy had found an excellent translator, the same one who had come to translate for every group who came to Ashley for education or treatment, and he did an extraordinary job. Nothing was lost in translation, because of the translator's skill of course, but primarily because of the universality of the message. There was electricity in that room when Father finished his address.

Within three years, Father's reputation in Russia had grown to such a degree that there was a group in St. Petersburg named after him. On one of our return trips, Father asked about one of the artists he had met, a highly talented and renowned musician. Father was informed that he had again begun to drink. Father just looked at me and my wife, Gini, and said, "We've got to make a call," and that's exactly what we did.

The next year, Father made his third trip to Russia and it was, Lou Bantle recalls, "a big one."

It had taken us five years to arrange a meeting with His Holiness Alexei II, the Patriarch of Russia. After attending a liturgy at which the Patriarch presided on the Feast of the Assumption in the Cathedral of the Assumption, one of five cathedrals within the walls of the Kremlin, we had a private audience with him. It was at that meeting that he gave his verbal blessing to the work the International Institute was doing and opened the doors of Russian Orthodox churches to A.A. meetings. It was a wonderful day for us.

Even today Father Martin's is probably one of the few names that is recognized immediately among those who offer treatment for alcoholism in Russia. And despite the centuries-old schism that exists between the Roman Catholic Church and the Russian Orthodox Church, as a result of the meeting that Father Martin had with the Patriarch, any program or meeting in Russia that is in any way affiliated with Father Martin has the full support of the Russian Orthodox Church. During Father's last trip to Russia, he addressed the Theological Academy in St. Petersburg, and when he was finished he received, as usual, a standing ovation.

Between trips to Russia, Father was invited to Switzerland to speak at the tenth anniversary of an English-speaking A.A. group

238

in Lausanne. Father then traveled to Poland, where it had been arranged for him to speak to several hundred counselors in training. He then addressed the faculty and students of the psychology department at the Catholic University of Lublin, the one university that had remained "free" in the Communist-controlled country. "I knew that the University had remained open because of the efforts of Pope John Paul II," Father recalls, "and I was especially honored when I learned that the president of the University was present at my lecture."

Honors, accolades, awards, and invitations to address major conferences continued to pour into Ashley. In 1993, while Father and Tommy were on vacation in Florida, Mae called Father and told him to sit down because she had some very exciting news for him. For the previous six years, the Vatican had held an annual international conference on a major health problem, and this year, the topic was to be alcoholism and drug addiction. Mae informed Father that he had been invited to participate. Father accepted, of course; Mae recalls that he was ebullient over the prospect of traveling to Rome and seeing the Vatican. Alex Abraham and several of Ashley's board members, including Lou Bantle and his family, Ralph Rossi, and Jim Cassidy, would accompany Father on the trip. (In fact, it was Lou Bantle who had told the American Ambassador to the Vatican, Thomas Malady, about Father Martin's success in the field of alcoholism recovery, and this contact resulted in the invitation for Father to participate.)

As the date of the conference approached, Father began to feel anxious about his presentation. He had been told that there would be 11 people on his panel and that the entire panel had a total of an hour and a half. "It didn't take me too long to figure out I only had about six minutes to speak, allowing time for introductions" Father recalls,

> and I began to realize that I really had my work cut out for me. I talked it over with Mae, and although she wanted me to deliver a version of the Chalk Talk, we both agreed there just wasn't

Father Martin with His Holiness Alexei II, the Patriarch of Russia. (Courtesy of Mr. Lou Bantle.)

enough time. We finally agreed that I should make a tape recording of what I wanted to say, and we could shorten it from there. As I listened to the recording, I began to realize that in my comments I had returned to the essence of sobriety: the Twelve Steps. So I decided to concentrate on that.

Father's presentation was—as always—appropriate and inspiring, particularly since one of the speakers who preceded him spoke for so long that the chair of the panel had to tap on his microphone repeatedly to get him to stop. Father drew an analogy between the donkey that had carried Christ into Jerusalem on Palm Sunday and A.A.: "No one knows the name of that donkey; it is anonymous—just as the names of the millions of people in A.A. are anonymous—we are the donkeys of the world who have been chosen by God to carry the message of sobriety to God's other wounded children." Father then explained that, given his time constraints, he need not list the Twelve Steps; instead, he could give the "shorthand" version that he had learned so many years ago from Dr. Bob through Austin Ripley: "Trust God, Clean House, Help Others."

Father Martin is too modest to tell anyone about the audience's response to his presentation, but Lou Bantle loves to tell everyone: "There were two people who got a standing ovation throughout that three-day conference, and one of them was the Pope."

From the moment Lou Bantle arrived in Rome, he had done everything he could to arrange for Father Martin to have an audience with Pope John Paul II. Lou recalls:

> We were contacting everyone we could in order to arrange for the audience, but we had no way of knowing if we would succeed until one day, near the end of our visit, about 5:00 in the evening, I got a phone call from the Ambassador's office saying that we were all invited to the Vatican the next morning at 8:00 when the Pope would be celebrating Mass in his private chapel; Father would be one of the co-celebrants.
>
> Jim Cassidy and I went immediately to Father's room to give him the news. I will not forget his reaction for as long as I live. Father Martin started to cry; he was so overcome with joy and gratitude. He just sat on the bed and rocked back and forth with tears in his eyes. "I can't believe this," he kept saying, when he was finally able to talk.
>
> Well, Father Martin got only a bit of sleep that night. At two in the morning, he got up, showered, and shaved. He read the Divine Office for the day, said his rosary, and waited for the sun to rise.
>
> Jim Cassidy had decided that we couldn't risk getting caught in Roman traffic on our way to the Vatican, so he had informed us all the night

before that we had to be outside the hotel at 6:00 for the car ride. It didn't take us too long to figure out that there is very little traffic in Rome at 6:00 in the morning, so we were at the Bronze doors of St. Peter's Basilica at the Vatican in about five minutes.

The place was deserted, except for one old woman feeding the pigeons. We just stood there, needling Jim, but Father was in awe, and we could tell that he was very nervous.

At about 7:00 a young priest came along who was also going to celebrate the Mass, and we began to talk to him. He told us that he was a recovering alcoholic who had found his sobriety at Guest House. Father couldn't get over the coincidence of it, but after all the efforts I had made to arrange for this meeting, I just had to know how the young priest had managed to get an invitation. "I wrote and asked," he said. Talk about the power of the written word.

In any event, when we finally entered the Pope's chapel, we were overwhelmed by the beauty and sanctity of the occasion, and Father Martin went to prepare for Mass with the other priests who would be celebrating. Father sat directly to the left of the Pope—I have never seen him so happy; I really never have.

After the Mass, we all went into a large conference room, and the Pope came around, shook the hand of each person present, and gave each of us a mother-of-pearl rosary. We have a picture of Father shaking the Pope's hand, and his face is like that of a child in awe. It's easy for us to forget that Father has lived his entire life serving God through the Church, but it was apparent to us all that day. There was nothing anyone could offer to him that would even come close to matching that

moment when he shook Pope John Paul's hand.
Those of us who knew Father Martin were cry-
ing with joy at the sight of him—it's a moment
I'll never forget.

When Father Martin returned to Ashley from Rome, he told
the patients about his experience meeting Pope John Paul II of
course, but he used the occasion not as an opportunity to talk
about his own good fortune, but to help the patients understand
what Austin Ripley had taught him more than 30 years before:
the one thing that every recovering alcoholic can be sure of is
that life will improve with sobriety.

Father Martin held himself up to the patients at Ashley as an
example of this. He asked the patients to look at the direction his
life had taken as a result of his sobriety: he had been able to serve
God as a Catholic priest, he had met Mae and Tommy, he and
Mae had started Ashley where thousands of people had found
sobriety, and most wonderful of all, he had met the Pope, his spiritual leader on Earth. As Austin Ripley had promised in one of
the letters he had written shortly after Father Martin left Guest
House, "Your past is discharged, your present secure, and your
future assured." Father used his own life as a promise to his
patients: they, too, could enjoy the fruits of sobriety, and he
promised as well to pray for them every day of his life.

Many of those former patients—and there are thousands of
them—pray for Father Martin. They also call him; visit him; send
him donations; ask him to care for their friends, relatives, and co-
workers at Ashley as he has cared for them; and write to him to
tell him how well they are doing as a result of their stay at Ashley.
To these people, Father Martin is a celebrity, but even more
important, he is the person who helped them to find sobriety. Pat
Hitchcock estimates that hundreds of people communicate in
person, by phone, or by letter with Father each year, and she
notes, "Father does his best to respond to every one of them."

Father Martin values each of these expressions of gratitude and
support, but there is one letter, written by Kevin Thornton, a former patient at Ashley, that best reflects the essence of Father

"Certainly one of the happiest days of my life," says Father Martin of his meeting with Pope John Paul II. (Courtesy of Father Martin.)

Martin's Ashley. The letter was addressed to Karen Roberts, Kevin's aunt; it was she who had recommended Ashley to him. It is reprinted here with Kevin's permission.

Dear Aunt Karen,

I was walking home from a meeting tonight, easing along the cracked sidewalks, doing what I normally do when I walk—looking straight up at the sky. I'm always searching the darkened skies these days for stars, a habit I picked up while at Ashley. That's what made me think of you, and of Father Martin, so I thought I'd give these thoughts a shot.

While I was at Ashley, I stood one cold, clear night on the back porch of the solarium, smoking a cigarette, taking a break from my work on the Fourth Step. I was staring straight up that night, feeling the endless black sky, following the dots of stars to infinity. A thought crossed my mind just then, a thought about shooting stars, and how rare they are to see. Like a paintbrush stroke across the sky, a shooting star passed directly through my vision, just like that, a passing second, and the hand of God touched the sky before me.

That's why I look at the sky nowadays. Not so much searching for shooting stars, but reminding myself of where I've been, and where I'm going. And thinking often of Ashley, where I'm sure God lingers on cold autumn nights. When I look at the sky, way above the cracked sidewalks and traffic on my level, it's the same sky I saw that night at Ashley. No matter where I am standing, I need only look up and see the same perspective, the same sky, the same hope that I saw that night.

All of that I say because it reminds me so much of Father Martin. His hand was there that night too, as it was those 30 days at Ashley, and ever remains. The beauty of that moment was that it was possible because Father Martin told a deathly scared alcoholic one afternoon to "get in here right away and start getting well." And from that moment until now I've only seen Father Martin a handful of times, but his touch is imbedded on me.

That's his beauty. He may be a speaker and a fund-raiser and a film personality, but in the matter of carrying out God's will, he is quiet and determined and behind the scenes. His is a gift given freely and given often, but one not needing constant recognition.

When I think of Father Martin, I think of his repugnance at the phrase "tough love," and his own philosophy of compassion and caring for the alcoholic, manifested in places like Ashley, and in people all over the world who have been touched by his kindness and simple caring of others like himself.

That's why I think of the stars again. Because I was standing in that place at that moment, because Father Martin had cared about me. Didn't know me, had never met me, but took my phone call and told me straight away that he cared, and he understood, and that he had a place for me. All of that meant more than words can describe . . . it meant for me my life.

So when I think of Father Martin, I think of the simple things. I think of the things I've gotten back in my life—my dignity and self-esteem, my family and job, my desire to see others as people instead of annoyances, my great desire to share what I have been given so freely.

I think it's those simple things that Father Martin instilled in me quietly. He simply let me know they were there for the taking with some work and acceptance. He said it quietly, without pressure, then went about the business of helping others like myself.

For him, it is a quiet mission, and I cannot imagine how many others carry a special moment or place for Father Martin with them. I know I do, and always will.

In the fall of 1994, Mae decided to celebrate Father's seventieth birthday with a surprise party at Ashley. Father was indeed surprised when he walked into the dining room and saw almost 200 people waiting to sing "Happy Birthday" to him. A large banner read: "Congratulations on the 30th Anniversary of Your 40th Birthday." Leonard had arranged for 15 people to "roast" Father: his brother, Edward; Father Tom Clark, with whom Father had taught at St. Charles; Hal Tulley (who remembered that the seminarians loved it when Father Martin was in charge of study hall because he would always fall asleep); Alex; Rick Esterly, with whom Father had worked for the state of Maryland; Geraldine Delaney, the director of Alina Lodge, who at 88 told Father that he was still just a boy; Conway Hunter; Jamie Carraway; Mary Jane Noble, who recalled how her husband had fallen in love "with a fellow Irishman with his charming ways"; Lou and Gini Bantle, who despite Mae's insistence that there be no gifts, donated $70,000 to the Scholarship Fund—a thousand dollars for each year of Father's life; Thomas Henderson, the former Dallas Cowboy's linebacker, who told the audience he had learned from Father that "we are not our mistakes, we are who we've become"; and board members Jim Cassidy, Mike Deaver, and Robert Johnson.

Despite the speakers' best attempts, it was not much of a "roast" after all; each concluded that Father had changed and in some cases saved their lives. As Jamie Carraway said, "I've spent the last two weeks trying to think of 'roasting' stories, but I remember acts of kindness and generosity instead."

Perhaps Mike Deaver best described the effect that Father Martin's life and work has had on the thousands of alcoholics

Tammy Wynette serenades Father Martin at his seventieth birthday party.
(Courtesy of Father Martin.)

who have received treatment at Ashley when he told the following story:

> I went to work about two years ago at an office at 13th and K streets in Washington, D.C., and there's a little coffee shop right on the corner named Patty's. The fellow who works in the office next to me came in after I'd been there about three weeks and he said, "You know, I went into Patty's this morning and Patty said, 'there's a guy who comes in here all the time now who looks exactly like Mike Deaver.' And I told her, 'that is Mike Deaver.' And she said, 'No, no, no, this isn't Mike Deaver.' And I said, 'I know it's Mike Deaver; I work in the office right next to him.' She said, 'It couldn't be Mike Deaver. This is a nice guy.'"
>
> I tell you this story because Father Martin changed my life and changed me. When I came to Ashley, I had been with presidents and kings and popes and prime ministers, but Father was the most powerful person I had ever met, and he still is today. You see, Father has the power to change people, to make them better, to make them whole again.
>
> I want to thank you, Father, for what you've done to me.

In 1995 Mae, Tommy, and Father decided, Mae recalls, "that we weren't getting any younger." Mae was fond of saying that "they were replacing A.A. with A.A.A.—aging, ailing, and aching." Mae was particularly concerned with Father's discomfort as he climbed the stairs of their home several times a day to get to and from his room. As a result, "buildingitis" struck again. This time, Mae decided to sell the home that she, Tommy, and Father had lived in for almost 25 years in order to move to a one-story house less than a mile away.

Father Martin and Mae Abraham in 1996. (Courtesy of Mrs. Mae Abraham.)

Some people predicted that it would take a year before all the renovations that Mae wanted could be complete, but those weren't the people who had watched Mae transform Ashley from a dilapidated estate to one of the most magnificent facilities in the United States. The renovations were completed in less than four months, and as a result, Mae explains proudly to her guests, "Father doesn't have to climb stairs anymore."

Mae celebrated her sixty-ninth birthday soon after they moved into the new house, but she still arrives at Ashley every morning at 8:30, after having spoken with Leonard at 7:00 to go over the day's agenda. Although Father Martin may be known as the finest communicator in the field, Mae holds her own. After delivering a lecture about Ashley and her work in April of 1996, Mae received the following thank-you note from her good friend, Charles Mullen, Director of the Baltimore County Bureau of Substance Abuse.

Dear Mae,

The rave notices are still coming in! I can't remember when we had a speaker who commanded such rapt attention from the group.

For years I've been hearing a dozen versions of the origins of Ashley, some of them close to the truth but always just a little bit off the mark. You were able to set the record straight beautifully. The second thing that people have been commenting on is that, placed in context, the Ashley story is really inspirational. It's the story of the Higher Power working through two drunks of diametrically opposed backgrounds (not unlike those of Bill and Bob), groping their way toward a goal which neither of them perceived clearly at the time. The net result is Ashley as it stands today, and I think we can all feel, vicariously, the sense of gratitude coupled with achievement that you and Father feel today.

Thanks again for coming down, Mae. And my very best regards to himself, Sir Joseph of Martin.

During the summer of 1996, Father Martin received yet another invitation to speak to a group of recovering alcoholics, but this one was very special. It was a request to address the alumni of Guest House on the occasion of its fortieth anniversary. The significance of the invitation was not lost on Father. It was at Guest House, 38 years before, where he had found his sobriety, where he had met Austin Ripley and Dr. Walter Green, where he had learned about the Twelve Steps, and where he had first spoken the words, "My name is Joe Martin, and I'm an alcoholic." And it was at Guest House where the seeds of Ashley were first planted. Now, of the thousands of priests who had found sobriety at Guest House, it was Father Martin who had been chosen to address his fellow recovering priests on this special occasion.

Father did not prepare a speech as he had for the Vatican conference on alcoholism. "If there were ever an occasion when I would speak from the heart," he says,

> then speaking to my fellow priests about Rip and Guest House was that occasion. You could even say that everything I had done for the past 38 years, from the moment I left Guest House, had prepared me for this speech. There are very few of us priests left who were at Guest House while Rip was alive, so I decided that I would try to speak for him, to help those who had benefitted from his lifelong labor of love to understand the depth of his devotion to alcoholic priests.

When Father Martin had first traveled to Guest House in 1958, he was only 33 years old, and he had flown to Lake Orion, Michigan, by himself, afraid, despondent, and unable to imagine that he could ever regain the respect of his family, his fellow priests, and his superiors. Thirty-eight years later, Father traveled to Rochester, Minnesota, where Guest House is now located, but this time, he was accompanied by Hershel Blackburn, a good friend and Ashley employee who travels everywhere with him now to ensure his safety and comfort. Father was no longer afraid and ashamed; instead, he had achieved a reputation, not only as the co-founder of one of the most highly respected treatment centers in the world, but also as one of the most renowned speakers in the field of alcoholism.

It was not as a celebrity that Father addressed the hundreds of priests who had gathered to celebrate Guest House's anniversary and to hear him speak, however; it was as a fellow priest, as a fellow alcoholic. "I'm Joe Martin," he said as he stood at the podium, "and I'm an alcoholic."

The priests who heard him that evening did not hear a version of the Chalk Talk, or a version of any of the other highly effective lectures that Father has composed and delivered. Father was speaking to men who had, like him, devoted their lives to the Church, the very men for whom Austin Ripley had established

Guest House. This was, perhaps, the most special audience Father had ever addressed, and Father's talk was most special as well.

Father was 71 years old; his once-bright red hair had turned completely white; he had gained weight; he did not walk with the same quick stride as he once had. But on that evening, speaking to alcoholic priests from all over the United States, Father Martin gave the performance of his life.

As always, he began with a few jokes, many of them self-deprecating, referring to his age and loss of agility. He recounted his own struggle with alcohol as a young priest, and he seemed to be speaking for the sake of the young priests in the audience, helping them to understand that he, too, had been there, knew the feelings of fear and despair and loneliness.

He talked about Rip and Doc Green of course, and he explained that everything he had done subsequent to his stay at Guest House he had done in gratitude "for what God has given me. The ability to be able to pass on to others what I've learned from Rip and Doc has been the singular most wonderful blessing of my life."

And of course, he talked about Mae, "the woman who saved my life, the woman who saves lives every day with her wisdom, her kindness, and her determination." And he talked as well about the importance of his vocation: "We especially will know the gift of our priesthood," Father said, "because the gift has been returned to us through our sobriety—those of us who have lost something can truly appreciate its value after it has been returned to us."

Father spoke for almost 40 minutes, and toward the end of his address, he grew serious, even somber, and said,

> I am not a fatalist, but I must be realistic. I will be fertilizing daisies in a few years. Ashley is in excellent hands: we have the most wonderful staff of highly trained and dedicated people in the world.
>
> But I don't like to think of Ashley without a priest. So I invite those of you who still have some hair on your heads to come and visit us. You

253

Tommy and Audrey Abraham sit beside Father Martin at Mae and Tommy's 50th wedding anniversary celebration. (Courtesy of Mrs. Mae Abraham.)

have had the Guest House experience, so you know first-hand the model that Ashley tries to follow. See for yourself the way Mae and I have taken all that I learned at Guest House and from Rip and used it to help anyone who comes to us. Maybe you'll decide to stay and take my place.

Father meant what he said: he knew that he, Mae, and Leonard would not live forever, and just as they had made other arrangements for the future, he wanted to make the necessary "spiritual" arrangements as well. He knew, not only as a result of his own experiences but as a result of the experiences of the thousands of alcoholics he had met throughout his life, that unless the spiritual needs of alcoholics are met, their recovery will not be complete.

Father's final words to his brother priests were the same words that Rip had used so often when trying to express his emotions to fellow alcoholics: "The tongue is mute when it is faced with the impossible task of expressing the simplest feelings of the heart." After a second or two of silence, during which the audience absorbed Father's words, there followed a five-minute stand-

Mae, Alex, and Tommy Abraham at Mae and Tommy's 50th wedding anniversary celebration. (Courtesy of Mrs. Mae Abraham.)

ing ovation. Father stepped down from the podium, returned to his seat, and blushed with pleasure as the applause continued.

In September of 1996, Mae and Tommy Abraham celebrated their fiftieth wedding anniversary. There was another surprise celebration—and this one was even more difficult to keep secret than the one celebrating Mae's sobriety had been.

This time, Pat arranged for Mae and Tommy to appear at a local hall where they thought Father and Alex would be receiving an award. In actuality, however, the hall was being set up for a dinner celebration for more than 200 guests. The dinner itself would be prepared at Ashley's kitchen and driven over to the nearby hall.

However, even though it was a Saturday, Tommy decided to stop in at Ashley, just to make sure everything was okay. When he saw the chef preparing huge trays of food and carrying them out to trucks parked behind the kitchen, Tommy was immediately suspicious. The chef managed to make up some excuse, but "it was a very close call," Pat Hitchcock recalls.

The dinner provided a perfect opportunity for Father Martin to thank Mae and Tommy, in public, for everything they had

Father Martin celebrates Mass in the Chapel. An inscription under the wreath reads, "Through death to life." (Courtesy of Mrs. Mae Abraham.)

done for him for the past 35 years. Father reflected as well on the truth of what Austin Ripley had told him so many years ago: "If you stay sober one day at a time, good things will happen in your life."

Mae and Tommy's anniversary dinner provided an opportunity for all of the people who had worked together for so long and so hard, with such good results, to realize the truth of those words. Mae and Tommy had struggled through the early years of their marriage until Father had helped Mae to find lasting sobriety. Mae and Tommy had helped Father to recover from his depression, inviting him into their home not as a guest, but as a family member. Together, they had worked so very hard to establish Ashley, joined by Leonard, and as a result of their hard work, they had found a labor that they loved to do. On that beautiful summer evening, it became apparent to everyone who was present that Mae and Tommy were absolutely happy not only because they were together, but because they were a part of something that was so much larger than they were.

Many years have passed since Father Joseph Martin met Mae and Tommy Abraham, and much has been accomplished—more than 10,000 patients have been treated at Ashley—but little has really changed. Mae still works far too hard and worries too much about Father, Tommy still does whatever he can to help Mae and Father at Ashley, and Father Martin is still happiest when he is helping alcoholics and drug addicts. As Father says, "I'll die with a piece of chalk in my hands, talking with a bunch of drunks and addicts."

No matter how many vacations Mae plans for Father, he is always happy to be home, anxious to get back to Ashley, to say Mass in the Chapel, to speak at the weekly graduation ceremony. Father Martin is invigorated by the presence of the patients at Ashley: it is when he is with them that he is most alive, most alert, most joyful. He knows recovering alcoholics and addicts need each other; this was one of the first things he learned from Rip, and it was one of the first things Rip learned from Bill Wilson and Dr. Bob Smith. It is the essence of recovery, the reason that Father ends every talk he gives with the words: "It's the likes of you that keep the likes of me going."

In 1959 Austin Ripley wrote a letter to Father praising him for the work he was just beginning to do. Even Rip, in all his wisdom, could not have known how prophetic his words would be: "What a truly magnificent contribution to life and to God lies before you," Rip wrote to his good friend. "Indeed what a wondrous thing God has wrought in your life. He is now preparing you for great things."